TRASHING
THE
PLANET

TRASHING THE PLANET

How Science Can Help Us Deal with Acid Rain,
Depletion of the Ozone, and Nuclear Waste
(Among Other Things)

DIXY LEE RAY
WITH
LOU GUZZO

HarperPerennial
A Division of HarperCollins*Publishers*

Chapter One, "Who Speaks for Science?" was adapted from an article originally appearing in *Imprimis*, Hillsdale College, August 1988, Vol. 17, No. 8; Chapter 5, "Acid Rain" was adapted from the article "The Great Acid Rain Debate" originally appearing in *The American Spectator*, January 1987.

A hardcover edition of this book was published in 1990 by Regnery Gateway. It is here reprinted by arrangement with Regnery Gateway.

HarperCollins books may be purchased for educational, business, or sales promotional use. For information, please call or write: Special Markets Department, HarperCollins Publishers, Inc., 10 East 53rd Street, New York, NY 10022. Telephone: (212) 207-7528; Fax: (212) 207-7222.

First HarperPerennial edition published 1992.

LIBRARY OF CONGRESS CATALOGING-IN-PUBLICATION DATA

Ray, Dixy Lee.
   Trashing the planet: how science can help us deal with acid rain,
depletion of the ozone, and nuclear waste (among other things) /
Dixy Lee Ray with Lou Guzzo.
     p.   cm.
   Originally published: Washington, D.C.: Regnery Gateway ; Lanham,
MD: Distributed by National Book Network, c1990.
   Includes bibliographical references and index.
   ISBN 0-06-097490-7 (paper)
   1. Pollution. 2. Environmental protection.
3. Human ecology. 4. Mass media and the environment.
5. Communication in science.
I. Guzzo, Louis R., 1919–   II. Title.
[TD174.R39 1992]   363.73—dc20   91-58526

92 93 94 95 96 CW 10 9 8 7 6 5 4 3 2 1

This book is dedicated to two groups of people. One, to all those honorable men and women of science and engineering, past and present, who work to better the conditions for human life on this planet. And, two, to all those sensible citizens who may wonder or worry what all the environmental fuss is about but whose access to facts is limited to the hyperbole of the popular media or to technical papers that are replete with qualifications and footnotes and are seldom written in common language. We have tried to be true to the first group while serving the second.

—DLR and LC

TABLE OF CONTENTS

Part Three
ISSUES NUCLEAR

Part Four
PARTING THOUGHTS

PREFACE

This book was written because I believe too many people are losing touch with common sense. Reading the headlines and lead stories in newspapers or listening to television and radio news, one could conclude that we Americans are the most gullible of people and certainly the most easily frightened. From simple scare stories about carcinogens lurking in everything we eat, breathe, and touch to truly stupendous claims of earth-destroying holes in the sky, global changes in climate, and doom for Western society, we have been panicked into spending billions of dollars to cure problems without knowing whether they are real.

Whatever happened to healthy skepticism? Whatever happened to the "show me before you spend my money" attitude? Shouldn't we question the assumption that *every* industrial product may be a danger to life and limb? Should *every* new development be fought against to protect us from everything, including ourselves?

I was delighted to read that an industrialist in England is fed up with always being on the receiving end of shocking allegations from opponents of progress. Norman Mischler, chairman of the British arm of the German chemical giant, Hoechst, hit back with this horrifying (but fictitious) account of the sinister goings-on at the plant of his "rival," Imperial Chemical Industries, about to market water as a fire-extinguishing agent. He wrote:[1]

ICI has announced the discovery of a new firefighting agent to add to their existing range. Known as WATER (Wonderful And Total Extinguishing Resource), it augments, rather than replaces, existing agents, such as dry powder and BCF (bromine-chlorine-fluorine), which have been in use from time immemorial. It is particularly suitable for dealing with fires in buildings, timber yards, and warehouses.

Though required in large quantities, it is fairly cheap to produce and it is intended that quantities of about a million gallons should be stored in urban areas and near other installations of high risk ready for immediate use. BCF and dry powder are usually stored under pressure, but WATER will be stored in open ponds or reservoirs and conveyed to the scene of the fire by hoses and portable pumps.

ICI's new proposals are already encountering strong opposition from safety and environmental groups. Professor Connie Barrinner has pointed out that if anyone immersed his head in a bucket of WATER, it would prove fatal in as little as three minutes. Each of ICI's proposed reservoirs will contain enough WATER to fill 500,000 two-gallon buckets. Each bucketful could be used 100 times, so there is enough WATER in one reservoir to kill the entire population of the U.K. Risks of this size, said Professor Barrinner, should not be allowed, whatever the gain. If the WATER were to get out of control, the results of Flixborough or Seveso would pale into insignificance by comparison. What use was a firefighting agent that could kill men as well as fire?

A local authority spokesman said that he would strongly oppose planning permission for construction of a WATER reservoir in this area, unless the most stringent precautions were followed. Open ponds were certainly not acceptable. What would prevent people falling in them? What would prevent the contents from leaking out? At the very least, the WATER would need to be contained in a steel pressure vessel surrounded by a leakproof concrete wall.

A spokesman from the fire brigades said he did not see the need for the new agent. Dry powder and BCF could cope with most fires. The new agent would bring with it risks, particularly to firemen, greater than any possible gain. Did we know what would happen to this new medium when it was exposed to intense heat? It had been reported that WATER was a constituent of beer. Did this mean that firemen would be intoxicated by the fumes?

The Friends of the World said that they had obtained a sample of WATER and found it caused clothes to shrink. If it did this to cotton, what would it do to men?

In the House of Commons yesterday, the Home Secretary was asked if he would prohibit the manufacture and storage of this lethal new material. The Home Secretary replied that, as it was clearly a major hazard, local authorities would have to take advice from the Health and Safety Executive before giving planning permission. A full investigation was needed and the Major Hazards Group would be asked to report.

If the United States were to be faced with such a new hazard as WATER, the Environmental Protection Agency would surely initiate public hearings and rule-making procedures that would drag the process out at least five years, cost several hundred million dollars, and end up regulating the use of WATER, requiring warning labels on WATER buckets, banning the sale of many common foods that contain WATER, and requiring the testing of all air meant for breathing, because it contains WATER vapor and it can be proved without doubt that too much oxygen is toxic.

Silly, isn't it? But that's essentially what we *are* doing with respect to many substances, particularly those that include man-made chemicals. Never mind that they are identical to "natural" chemicals. Whatever happened to common sense?

From the Luddites of the early days of the Industrial Revolution to the environmental extremists of today, opposition to the introduction of anything new has been a way to protect the status quo. Sometimes the opposition came from those whose livelihood was apt to be affected—as with the original Saboteurs, whose name derived from the tactic of throwing their wooden shoes—sabots—into the machines that were replacing them. Sometimes the opposition was rooted in ignorance and fear of the unknown, fear of what might happen. This probably explains the widespread belief early in this century in rural America that it was dangerous to use a telephone during a thunderstorm—because it could act as a conductor of lightning and "knock out the caller."

But if fear had won out, we wouldn't have had the Industrial Age or the world of high technology that we know today. We wouldn't have had the uneventful replacement of coal by oil, of thermal burners and furnaces by electrical processing, of vacuum tubes by transistors, of typewriters by word processors, of repetitive work by robotics, of manual design by computers, and so on. With today's more vocal opponents of technology, the motivation may be obscure, but the tactic is to frighten people of possible future consequences, however unlikely they may be.

This book is an effort to clarify environmental issues, to separate fact from factoid, to unmask the doom-crying opponents of all progress, and to re-establish a sense of reason and balance with respect to the environment and modern technology.

—D.L.R.   —L.R.G.

Part One

MAN, TECHNOLOGY, AND THE ENVIRONMENT

Chapter 1

WHO SPEAKS FOR SCIENCE?

I T IS NOW WIDELY ACCEPTED by the press and consequently by much of the general public that man's industrial activities are "fouling our nest" and pose a threat to the life of planet Earth, a threat that grows more ominous year by year. Is this conventional wisdom correct?[1]

The risk one runs in challenging so widely held a belief is the risk of being judged an apologist for industry, or worse, to be accused of favoring pollution. Now my disclaimer: I am not in the pay of nor am I employed by any industry and I am as much opposed to pollution as anyone. But I do part company with alarmists who misuse science to foment fear and who clamor with increasing stridency that industrial progress must stop or be redirected into uneconomic alternatives because the world is going to pot. Is it? Or is it that professional environmentalists and others whose jobs depend on the continuing environmental crises want us to think that all's wrong with the world?

A recent edition of Tacoma's daily newspaper, *The Morning News Tribune,* drew my attention with a headline on page one:[2] EPA PLANS TO PROBE SIMPSON MILL FOR DIOXIN. I was interested not only because the Simpson Mill (pulp and paper) is right here in my own "backyard" but because it was yet one more article on dioxin, one

3

of the scare substances we hear so much about. Why don't we look more closely at the question of whether it is truly dangerous, and if so, in what concentration?

I quote from the news article to make my point: "The national study was prompted in part by an investigation at the Tacoma mill last May, when EPA investigators caught nine flounder within 100 yards of the mill's underwater effluent outfall. Minute amounts of dioxin were found in the fish, according to the results of recent EPA tests."

As I read the article, I thought: For once a newspaper report has included an explanation of how much these "minute amounts" were and how they were detected. Much of the explanation, unfortunately, was buried in the continuation on the back page, but at least it was published.

This is what the reporter wrote. "The flounder contained 1.5 parts per trillion of TCDD, the most potent form of dioxin. Less toxic forms of the chemical were found from 0.2 parts per trillion to 3 parts per trillion. A part per trillion is equivalent to one drop in 25 million gallons."

Now, that's good, but how can anybody think such a small amount of a chemical could be harmful? The reporter went on to detail how the test was conducted:

"All nine flounder, including their internal organs, which normally contain high levels of pollutants, were blended together for testing."

Note that the 1.5 parts per trillion of dioxin were dispersed among the nine flounder, and that the test included the internal organs, which nobody ever eats, and the skin, which nobody ever eats. If ever there were a misleading way of making a test and laying it out for the public to see, there it is.

On the basis of a trivial 1.5 parts per trillion—not per flounder but in the total of nine flounder mashed up together, guts and all—the EPA proposed a national program to examine the aqueous environment around every pulp mill in the country! Well, that's one way to keep a job going and to keep spending public money.

On whose expertise did the EPA rely to decide that one ninth of 1.5 parts per trillion was a sufficient risk to human health to undertake an expensive and extensive nationwide program? It begs repetition of a question I have asked so often and have been trying to answer for many years: Who speaks for science? Or, to put it another way: On whom does the press rely to speak for science?[3]

Repeatedly over the last few years, the American public has been subjected to a litany of catastrophe, to predictions of impending disasters that are said to be unique to modern civilization. The oceans are dying, the atmosphere is poisoned, the earth itself is losing its capacity to support life.

Warnings that in the past came from the pulpit and called for eternal punishment in the sulfurous fires of hell have been replaced by equally dire predictions that come from alarmist environmentalists, who call for spending millions of taxpayer dollars in order to avoid doom from the sulfurous effluents of industry. The anticipated catastrophes are our own fault, of course, blamed on the greedy and perfidious nature of modern man.

Well, it's all pretty heady stuff, but is it true? As with so many issues that involve technology, the answer is "yes" and "no"—and probably rather more "no" than "yes"!

What are our real environmental concerns? Cancer-causing chemicals? Radiation, including radon? Carbon dioxide, ozone, the "greenhouse effect"? Each of them will be considered in some detail in later chapters, but a brief look now will help establish a perspective based on reason.

First, the cancer-causing chemicals. With the exception of childhood leukemia—always tragic, but relatively rare—cancer is a malady that afflicts predominantly older adults and the aged. For most cancers, and there are many different kinds, the causes are complex, interactive, and often include genetic factors. If we look at the fatality records, the facts show that the total of carcinogenic substances targeted by the EPA—including chemicals in the work place, environment, food additives, and industrial products—cause *fewer than eight percent of all cancer deaths in America.*[4]

The best scientific evidence points to genetics, viruses, sexual practices, diet, alcohol, and, more than anything else, tobacco, as accounting for nearly all of the remaining 92 percent. Yet, the public, through constantly reported innuendo against industrial chemicals and radiation, is encouraged to believe otherwise. Moreover, a proper look at cancer statistics shows that, aside from a sharp increase in lung cancer caused by cigarette smoking, there have been no significant increases in the rate at which people die from any of the common forms of cancer over the last 50 years. In fact, there have been significant decreases in some types of cancer—for example, stomach cancer—during these decades of rapid industrialization and the introduction of many new man-made chemicals.

But most people believe cancer is caused by toxic substances created by industry. Why? Because they listen to the wrong spokesmen, and that is all they hear.[5] National television has elevated sob-sister journalism to a new dramatic high, with emotional, heart-rending stories about cases of childhood leukemia and other individual or family tragedies as if they were epidemic. These stories capture public attention and play on natural sympathy, and these reactions, in turn, affect the decisions and budgets of governmental scientific agencies. In an internal memo, the Environmental Protection Agency (EPA) admits, with remarkable candor, "Our priorities [in regulating carcinogens] appear [to be] more closely aligned with public opinion than with our estimated risks."[6] And with scientific evidence, too, I hasten to add!

Now, as to the second example, radiation exposure, including radon, the simple fact is that we live in a radioactive world. We always have and we always will. Yet because a few scientists have made the unsubstantiated claim that *any* amount of radiation is harmful[7]—and that claim has been repeated often in the popular press—many have come to believe it.

Information about the essential and beneficial aspects of radioactivity, particularly in the thousands of lifesaving procedures in nuclear medicine, seldom reaches the public. Only the alarmists are heard. The negative effects of their warnings are serious, with increasing numbers of patients hesitant to accept radiation therapy. On the other hand, radon has become a national health problem because of our well meant but stupid insistence on sealing up our homes and buildings to conserve energy, without considering the possible ill effects.

As to the "greenhouse effect," it's true that the concentration of carbon dioxide in the atmosphere has been increasing. It is also true that the *rate* of the carbon dioxide increase—and methane, hydrocarbons, sulfur and nitrogen oxides, and a few other substances—is now approximately one percent a year. Since increases of carbon dioxide have also occurred in the geological past, without the help of human industry, it is unclear whether the burning of fossil fuel is the preeminent or only cause of the present increase, however much it may be adding to the current totals. Moreover, it is not known what the consequences may be, if any, of this increase, nor how long it may last. But this does not stop the doomsayers from hypothesizing radical climate transformations and other adverse effects in the future.[8]

We do *not* know what caused severe climatic changes in the geological past, but we can be sure they were *not* due to human industrial activity. Most likely, the causes were and still are colossal cosmic forces, quite outside human ability to control. Now that we live in an industrial, high technology society, there is no reason to believe that such cosmic forces have ceased to exist.

In these three areas of environmental concern (and in many others, including acid rain, the ozone layer, pesticides, and so forth), there is clearly a dichotomy between what is known and understood by the mainstream body of scientific experts and what the public believes because of the information it gets. But what the public believes to be true, even if it is wrong, has enormous consequences, since it is public opinion that determines how public funds are spent.

It seems so reasonable to conclude that once people understand how good and safe and environmentally benign a technology is, they will accept, if not welcome, it. It seems so reasonable to expect the public to be grateful for technologies that can mean improvement in environmental problems. But, alas, it doesn't work that way. Calm reason and alarmist environmentalism do not co-exist.[9]

The course of public events, especially in nuclear science and now increasingly in the chemical industry as well, has demonstrated over the last 10 to 15 years that scientists and engineers who speak on behalf of nuclear power and the chemical industry are not trusted. The public does not distinguish the Natural Resources Defense Council from the National Academy of Sciences and is far more likely to believe the opponents of science and technology than the supporters. If you are reluctant to accept that proposition, consider for a moment how a scientist would fare on 60 *Minutes*, or 20/20, or *Crossfire*, or on any of the many television and radio programs in which controversial issues, even highly complex technical ones, are treated in an adversarial, debate-like format, as if questions of scientific fact could be settled, not by evidence, but by argument.

I have likened this method of informing the public on scientific matters to a hypothetical situation in which a television program on criminal justice might feature a "balanced" panel made up of three judges and three criminals. That, of course, is being fair—presenting both sides. At least, that's the way it works in science and technology. In such a format, the opposition always "wins," because whoever is against any technology has only to make a charge, however preposterous, and doesn't have to prove it. That burden falls upon the supporter of science to prove that the charge is groundless. It is a difficult situation, and one that we tend to handle badly.

There was a time in my youth when reliable experts were believed. It was a time when most people and most institutions were presumed to be well-meaning and honest until and unless proved otherwise. It was also a time of unprecedented increase in our knowledge about the world, our belief in ourselves, and in our ability—through understanding and logic—to provide adequate solutions to technical problems. It was a time of optimism and progress. It was a time of improvement in our standard of living that made our society and our nation the envy of the world. It was a time when the use of knowledge was expected, when the myriad applications of science through technology made living on this planet easier and better, and gave us more time to enjoy it by increasing our life span beyond three quarters of a century.

Such progress continues, but it seems that hardly anyone enjoys it any more. Too many people have exchanged confidence for despair, too many have come to fear technology and to hate and reject anything nuclear or chemical-related. Despite all the evidence of our physical well-being beyond the dreams of all previous generations, we seem to have become a nation of easily frightened people—the healthiest hypochondriacs in the world!

What has brought this condition about? What has made us lament rather than rejoice? What has made us so quick to believe the worst about ourselves and so reluctant to recognize the good?

Among many possible explanations is this one: We have simply done a rotten job of teaching science. Oh, not to those students who will become scientists—we're quite good at that—but at the equally important job of teaching science to all those others, to the overwhelming 80 percent or more of the student population who will not enter science or engineering as a profession. There we fail miserably. The task of teaching science to non-majors is beneath the dignity of most academic scientists.

So now we must ask further: If not from the schools and colleges, where do most people get their information about science and about important applications of technology in modern society? The answer is easy: Mainly from television, and, to a lesser extent, from newspapers, radio, and news magazines. Who decides the content of this information? Not scientists, but reporters, news directors, and editors. Professor John Kemeny, chairman of the President's inquiry into the accident at Three Mile Island, commented after dealing with the press about his report:[10]

> I left Washington fully expecting to read the following story in one of our morning newspapers: "Three scientists, named Galileo, Newton, and Einstein, have concluded on the basis of their research that the earth is round. However, *The New York Times* has learned authoritatively that Professor John Doe of Podunk College has conclusive evidence that the earth is flat."

If we want a public that is better educated in science, more competent to judge who can be believed when speaking for science, and more able to make rational decisions on technical matters, then we must learn more about the different worlds in which scientists and reporters live and work. We have to recognize and accept that scientists, technologists, and engineers do not and can not inform the public directly. The media inform the public, and, in doing so, act as an information filter. The bottom line is that science and the media must learn to work together for a common purpose, because there is simply no other mechanism in a free society that can provide the necessary scientific information to voters and politicians. So far, unfortunately, this rapport between science and the media shows no signs of developing.[11]

Consider the differences in the ways of working, of motivation, and of rewards for scientists and for reporters. First, the scientists. For them, the volume of work is far less important than its quality. Scientists work at their own pace. There is no intractable daily or weekly deadline. Scientists work within a well recognized discipline, which is only a small part of the scientific whole. A scientist's work is judged by his peers, and unless it is peer-approved, it won't be published. For a scientist, all funding and professional advancement is based on peer-reviewed work. For all these reasons, therefore, scientists are very careful about making claims. Those who value their standing in their peer community will be cautious not to overstate, and they feel compelled to provide context for what they say. This is often interpreted by the non-scientific community as uncertainty, doubt, hedging, or as evidence of disagreement among scientists.

In the media, a reporter's key to advancement is the volume of his work, maximizing minutes of air time or inches of print. Competition for time and space is fierce. For the reporter, deadlines are externally imposed, short, and must be met. A reporter's work is judged, not by his peers, but by an editor or news director, and what attracts attention is of paramount importance. Good reporting is compact, without space for qualifications or context; on television, the usual maximum time for a report is one or two minutes, rarely more. Under such circumstances, reporters cannot search out and read scientific papers. Most of their work is done on the telephone and they seek out "experts" who will give them good one-liners.

There could hardly be two more disparate professions, and it is no wonder that misunderstandings and misrepresentations arise. Information flowing from the scientific environment to the media environment inevitably suffers alteration and filtration, and this affects what the public knows. In this regard, there appear to be three main problems.

The first one is *anxiety*. There is an understandable though unfortunate emphasis on the supposed conflict between technology and humanity. This makes good press, but provides a skewed perspective that heightens fear of science and technology.

The second is *factoids*—false, exaggerated, or misleading information that is made believable by constant repetition, such as PCBs cause cancer; organically grown food is more nutritious and healthier than if fertilizers and pesticides are used; any level of radiation is harmful; acid rain is caused by sulfur dioxide from coal-burning industry; and so forth.

There are dozens and dozens of such factoids—beliefs that have little or no evidence to support them. Some come about from the mistaken assumption that if two phenomena occur together or follow one another, they must represent cause and effect. Some come from a scientist desiring publicity for a cause or a political position. Some come from a zealous reporter trying to make a name for himself who intentionally or unintentionally distorts a scientific report.

The third problem is *misinterpretation*. Since good scientists limit their remarks within disciplinary boundaries and good reporters extrapolate into a broad or common context, the result is often misinterpretation. "I was misquoted," says the scientist, who vows never to talk to a reporter again. Such a reaction is a mistake because it leaves the important job of communicating with the media, and therefore with the public, to those scientists who are willing to take the chance of being misunderstood. Unfortunately, this all too often means scientists who avoid peer review for their work, have a mission or "cause," or are charlatans or quacks. Science has its quota of the latter, just as every profession does.

I realize that neither the media nor the nonscientists among us have the knowledge to judge the scientific community. Therefore, it's up to good scientists to weed out the phonies. That is not being done. Instead, such renegade organizations as the Union of Concerned Scientists and Physicians for Social Responsibility present themselves as the "voice of the scientific community." It is these organizations that support such "spokesmen for science" as Helen Caldicott, a pediatrician; Barry Commoner, a former geneticist; Paul Ehrlich, a butterfly specialist; Amory Lovins, a self-proclaimed physicist with no training, no degree, and no publications in that field; and many others who gain their reputation by attacking modern science and technology. It is the quasi- or pseudo-scientific or activist organizations whose backing enables such persons to pose as experts in matters of radiation, pesticides, and energy.[12] And our respected professional societies maintain a silent aloofness.

The scientific community judges very strictly its members who are at the top of their profession, but it ignores the incompetents and no-goods at the bottom. It is left to others of courage, like the Honorable Judge Patrick F. Kelly of the United States District Court in Kansas, to say, in November 1984, what scientists should have been saying all along:[13]

This court rejects the opinion testimony of Dr. Karl Morgan and Dr. John Gofman, because they both evince an intellectually dishonest invention of arguments to protect their opinion. . . . This is not a situation where the scientific community is equally divided between two respected schools of thought. It is a case where there is a small but very vocal group of scientists, including Dr. Morgan and Dr. Gofman, that holds views not considered credible by experts in the field. . . .

Remember, that was 1984. Dr. Morgan and Dr. Gofman are still making a very good living as consultants and court witnesses for anti-nuclear groups.

Dr. Ernest Sternglass, another person who is much quoted by the media on radiation matters, has never published his claims about the hazardous effects of low-level radiation in a peer-reviewed journal. In an article in *Esquire* magazine published in 1969, Dr. Sternglass predicted that all children in the U.S. would die as a result of fallout from nuclear tests in the atmosphere. Many years have passed, and—unfortunately for his credibility but fortunately for the children—he was and is wrong. But his opinions, long since dismissed by knowledgable scientists in his field, are still actively sought and quoted by the popular press.

Until respected scientists, preferably through their professional societies and preferably backed up by the National Academy of Science and the National Academy of Engineering, identify the purveyors of misrepresentation, they have only themselves to blame for fear, misunderstanding, the persistence of factoids, and the rejection of technology.

Scientists should be very jealous of who speaks for science, particularly in our age of rapidly expanding technology. The learned organizations of scientists and engineers should work to become the pre-eminent spokesmen for science. Only one, the Scientists and Engineers for Secure Energy (SE2), is doing this on a planned and consistent basis, but only on energy issues. Why doesn't the American Nuclear Society speak up—as an organized, respected representative of the thousands of nuclear experts? Is it because of an excess of timidity?

Of course, we must acknowledge that competence in one field of science does not guarantee adequate information, understanding, or even objectivity in another. And we need to remember that while assessing data and drawing conclusions drawn from the evidence is obviously a job for scientists, taking a position on the possible or likely social consequences of adopting some technology is a job for citizens and politicians. The former demands expert technical knowledge; the latter does not.

Final decisions are made, quite rightly, by the people and their elected representatives. It is especially important, then, that responsible scientists and their institutions make sure that scientific facts get a proper airing in the media so that we can all make intelligent decisions about the new technologies and scientific issues that affect our lives.

Chapter 2

THE GOOD OLD DAYS?

T ECHNOLOGY, defined as the application of scientific knowledge to the solution of practical problems, has provided the
opportunity for improvement in the lives of all those people fortunate
enough to live in the advanced, industrialized, high-tech world that
we identify as Western civilization. No matter the recent blossoming of
awareness of nature; the natural world is a tough place in which to live.
I know. I was born into a world far more "natural" than today's. Let me
recall how it was 75 years ago. [1]

The world in which I spent my early years was a very smelly place.
The prevailing odors were of horse manure, human sweat, and un-
washed bodies. A daily shower was unknown; at most there was the
Saturday night bath.

Indoors the air was generally musty and permeated by the sweetly
acrid stench of kerosene lamps and coal fires. It was the era of the horse
and buggy, the outhouse, and dirt. Depending upon the weather, it was
either dusty or muddy. Only a few urban streets were paved—with
cobblestones or brick. Mud puddles and corrugated ruts or "corduroy
roads" were the potholes of my youth.

Automobiles had been invented, of course, but they were few in
number, handcrafted, and expensive enough so that only the rich

could afford them. I was nearly 10 years old when the Model T began to put America on wheels. Indeed, Mr. Henry Ford made a greater contribution to public health than most practitioners of science by introducing an affordable auto—which led to the eventual elimination of horse manure from public streets. I was still quite young when airplanes proved their worth in World War I. On rare occasions, especially during the summer, one could be heard overhead, and everyone rushed outside to marvel that something so big could actually fly! No one dreamed that air travel would one day be taken for granted.

Long distance travel was by steam-driven train or boat. For shorter distances, one walked. In town were trolleys, first horse-drawn and then electric-driven. Most people did not venture far from home.

Electrification of cities and homes was much talked about. Gas lights were slowly being replaced with electric lights. But the "gas works" that burned coal and produced manufactured gas persisted for decades and fouled the city atmosphere. Electricity in the home usually meant a single 15 or 25 watt light bulb hanging from a wire in the center of a room. No matter where you stood or what you did, you were nearly always in your own shadow. I remember the first free-standing table lamp in our home. It was 1922, and I was 8 years old.

It was a long time before electricity extended to household appliances. There were no electric refrigerators or freezers. Food was kept in a "cooler" or an icebox. The latter was a great improvement, especially for meat and dairy products, but it worked because the ice melted. This meant the accumulation of water in a "drip pan" under the icebox; it was a small daughter's chore to empty that pan every day without spilling it.

There were no thermostats in the home of my childhood. Furnaces were replacing fireplaces as the main heating unit. The furnace burned wood or coal. One learned very young how to bank the fire for the night, how to shake down the ashes, and, in the case of coal, how to remove the klinkers. Rotten duty!

The world I was born into had no electric irons or toasters and no vacuum cleaners. We used brooms and carpet beaters and muscle. There were no electric washing machines or dryers, only tubs that could be heated on the kitchen stove. A scrubbing board, hand wringer, and clothes line completed the equipment for washing clothes. Such things as an automatic dishwasher, food processor, or microwave were unknown.

There was no radio, no television, no VCR. Music, other than that from instruments played by family members, came from a hand-cranked record-playing machine, called a "Victrola." There was no air conditioning. Telephones existed but no satellite communications, no word processors, no calculators, no computers, no electronics. Business machines consisted of a hand-cranked "adding machine" and a manual typewriter. There were no plastics, no ceramics, no pre-stressed concrete structures, and no synthetic fibers.

The very first man-made thread was rayon, introduced about 1927. Cloth, for clothing and other purposes, was made only from natural fibers, cotton, wool, silk, and linen. Imagine trying to clothe people today with only those fibers available. As it was, most people had few clothes; that is, few changes. It was common to own only two sets, one for "every day" and one for Sunday or "dress up."

I could go on and on. But permit me, instead, to turn to two fields wherein the differences between my youth and today—and the improvement and progress—have been truly dramatic: food production and medicine.

When I was young, fresh food could be eaten only when in season. Some fruits and vegetables could be preserved by canning, but the processes for safe home canning were poorly understood and unreliable. Food poisoning was common. Every year people were stricken with botulism and salmonella or various digestive upsets caused by eating decayed or tainted food. During the winter, therefore, only potatoes, carrots, cabbage, winter squash, onions, and dried beans were generally available. Some people ate rutabagas, turnips, and parsnips, but, in our family, these were considered "horse food." Only with the introduction of widespread refrigeration of rail cars and boats, warehouses, and grocery food containers could fresh food be brought to the customer throughout the year.

Refrigeration vastly expanded the market for all foods—meat, dairy products, fruits and vegetables—and that required that more food be grown. The remarkable productivity of American farmers depends in no small degree on the proper use of artificial fertilizers, herbicides, and pesticides. Improved production technology and good management have made it possible to reduce the amount of land devoted to growing food by more than 450 million acres.

As Dr. Norman Borlaug has said, "Without the availability and proper use of chemical fertilizers, herbicides, insecticides, and fungicides, the worldwide demands for food cannot be met."

Certainly they have improved the nutrition and diet of people in America, and astonishing as this change has been, it is equalled or excelled by the improvements in medicine and health.

Infectious childhood diseases were a fact of life during my youth. Epidemics were common and most families were familiar firsthand with whooping cough, measles, mumps, pneumonia, diphtheria, scarlet fever, chicken pox, and more. Body lice causing a severe itch, called the "seven-year itch" (which has taken on a very different connotation in recent decades), infested schools and their inhabitants. In my home town, the last smallpox epidemic was recorded in 1923–24. Poliomyelitis, or polio, for which there was no preventative and no treatment, was called infantile paralysis. It left many children crippled or confined for life in an "iron lung." I was in junior high school when polio last hit many of my classmates. Then there was an ailment known as "brain fever," probably meningococcus infection, for which there were no antibiotics. Many children suffered something we called "growing pains." It wasn't a TV program; it was childhood rheumatism, and it left its victims with hearts that were weakened for life.

If one survived childhood diseases, and many did not, there was always "galloping consumption" or tuberculosis waiting for young adults. So common was "TB" that most communities had a special hospital called a sanatorium for its victims.

I grew up in a "goiter belt" and remember when adults, especially women, were often afflicted and grew enormous swellings of the throat. This unsightly malady was cured by a simple expedient, one of the first introductions of a chemical into the diet—in this case, the element iodine—by adding it to common table salt.

The control, and in many instances the virtual elimination, of childhood infectious diseases has come about through the use of medical technology. It is a good thing. Now, of course, we can direct our worry and hand-wringing against cancer.

The improved health that results from a better understanding of physiology, biochemistry, nutrition, and pharmaceuticals has led to a longer and healthier life. The belief that the "good old days" were simple, benign, and kind is *wrong!* The reality is those days were dirty, disease-ridden, and smelly.

When this century began, human life was almost totally dependent upon the whims of uncaring nature and the availability of already existing natural resources. This is no longer true. In the last 50 years, we have seen more of a gain in human independence and more changes in the way humans live and what humans can do than occurred in all human history up to the twentieth century. We have been privileged to live through the most extraordinary five decades of expanding knowledge and its use for bettering life that the world has ever known. Little wonder that some people cannot cope. Our challenge now is to ensure that we be informed and sensible stewards of this planet and all its life.

Chapter 3

IT WORKS BETTER IF YOU PLUG IT IN

IN MANKIND'S LONG PATH of progress out of savagery into today's technological society, a few major achievements stand out.

The journey started with energy, when humans learned how to use fire. Our ability to control fire has never been complete or perfect, though there has been great progress in the development of fire retardant materials and smoke detectors (the latter dependent on the radioactive element, americium, to be effective). Even so, many lives are lost and much property damage occurs every year from uncontrolled fires.[1]

Fire, like a nuclear warhead, can be used as a weapon of mass destruction. Recall that more people, more civilians, were killed in the fire-bombing of Tokyo than in the nuclear bombings of Hiroshima and Nagasaki. Civilian casualties suffered during the fire-bombing of Dresden totaled 300,000. The deaths, both immediate and delayed, from the combined atomic detonations at Hiroshima and Nagasaki were under 250,000. Still, we continue to use fire for important, even essential, applications.

Fire and its use permitted primitive men to extend the variety and improve the nutritional quality of foods. Cooking makes cereal grains more digestible and can destroy the natural toxicity present in many vegetables. Fire enlarged the range of habitable climates by providing warmth. In a broad sense, the ability to use fire led to the development of agriculture and animal husbandry, from which cooperative settlements and cities grew.

The ability to use fire also led to the development of charcoal and made metal-working possible, which, in turn, expanded our knowledge of minerals and ores. Aside from human and animal muscle power, the burning of wood was the prime energy of civilization for 5,800 of the 6,000 years of known human history. Of course, there was some use of wind for driving ships, and both wind and moving water were used to grind grain and for a few mechanical applications.

Then, only 200 years ago, there began a rapid expansion in the use of burning materials—first coal, then natural and manufactured gas. Eventually, petroleum became the driving energy for the industrial revolution. Each fuel replaced the previous one, not because of resource shortages, but because each replacement fuel was better, easier to use, and more efficient. It has been our growing knowledge and use of electricity since the 1880s that has made the use and advancement of technology possible. [2]

With electricity, anyone, by pushing a button or turning a switch, can command power that was once unknown, unbelievable, and unavailable even to princes, potentates, and high priests of all the ages past. Yet we do not wonder, in awe, at this miraculous power, even though all that we call "high technology" is electricity-dependent. What Thomas Edison said of the light bulb is also true of the computer: "It works better if you plug it in." [3]

Electricity powers word processors, business machines, and robotics. Electricity fuels advanced industrial processes and financial transactions. Electricity makes modern communications possible, from television to telephones to satellite transmissions. Electricity runs all the equipment that takes the drudgery out of domestic life.

Considering domestic life, what woman would give up her electric washing machine for a scrubbing board, her electric dryer for a hand-wringer and clothes line, her vacuum cleaner for a carpet beater and broom, her air conditioner and furnace for a wood- or coal-burning stove? Electricity has done more to liberate women than all the speeches and protests and affirmative action programs that have often jolted our sensibilities. Indeed, technology has always had a liberating effect, nowhere more evident than with women.

The very first step taken to release women from true domestic bondage was the invention of the spinning wheel. It happened some time between the eleventh and twelfth centuries A.D., somewhere in Western Europe. Spinning had always been women's work. Weaving was done by men. Spinning involved the laborious winding of thread on a small stick called a "distaff" (hence the term "distaff" applied to the maternal family line). It took nine women with distaffs to keep one male weaver busy making cloth. But with a spinning wheel, one woman spinner could keep six weavers busy.

Woman's work, then, became valuable in the marketplace. For the first time in the Western world, a woman could keep the wealth she brought to a marriage (her dowry), own property in her own name, and, if she chose, support herself, rather than depend upon a husband; hence, the term, "spinster," for a woman who is not married.

For a long time after the introduction of the spinning wheel, there was little real progress in the social and economic position of women until the industrial revolution brought three new technical inventions—the sewing machine, the typewriter, and the telephone, all of which opened new avenues for the employment of women.

Today, with the electrification of the home and the science and technology that has made physical strength no longer a determining factor in many jobs, women are freer to do what they will. How ironic it is that it is still considered more appropriately feminine in some quarters for women to be anti-technology.

Obviously, science, technology, industrialization, and electricity, have not brought us Utopia. But it is most certainly true that in the industrialized, electricity-driven, technology-based world, people live longer and healthier lives, have greater relief from drudgery and hard manual labor, enjoy a greater share of goods and services, have more mobility, and enjoy more personal liberty than has ever before been experienced on Earth. Given an average life expectancy that exceeds 75 years, we must be doing something right—junk food, nuclear waste, and all.

Certainly we have to acknowledge that technology has sometimes had unexpected side effects. People worry about new technologies, usually when possible side-effects (however improbable they may be) are dwelt upon to the exclusion of the possible benefits of the new technology. Perhaps it has always been so. I quote from *The Congressional Record*:

> This begins a new era in the history of civilization. Never before has society been confronted with a power so full of potential danger and at the same time so full of promise for the future of man and for the peace of the world. The menace to our people . . . would call for prompt legislative action, even if the military and economic implications were not so overwhelming.

The year was 1857. The subject was not nuclear power but the internal combustion engine.

Our society today is technically advanced. I emphasize that because it is the hallmark of our age. Our society is based on knowledge and facts. It is not based on wishful thinking, though many well-meaning people wish it were. It is not based on emotion, even though some become emotional about certain issues. It is not based on compassion, concern, or sympathy, laudable as these noble sentiments may be. Nor is our society based on hysteria and protest. It is based on facts— verifiable, determinable, repeatable facts, developed through the intuitiveness of science and the pragmatism of technology. It is not a perfect society—only the best one ever invented.

Technology touches everyone. It permeates our lives. It establishes our standard of living. It affects our actions and decisions. All are influenced by scientific knowledge, its pursuit, and its use. Technology is uniquely and exclusively a human attribute. Who else makes machines and controls them?

True, the machines that man makes are like man himself: never perfect. It is also true that the direction and control of human inventions can be misguided or the results of knowledge misused, but these are human failings and therefore correctable. Technology is not, as some have asserted, a "thing" or "force" that has escaped from human control or that makes people do things they don't want to do. Technology encompasses a large number of many kinds of applications, developed by human minds and responsive to human control and direction.

Consider our view of electricity. Have we become so accustomed to using it that we sometimes forget where it comes from and how utterly dependent we are upon it? There are people still living in rural America who recall when electricity—just over a half-century ago in the 1930s—ushered in modern agriculture and began to relieve the farmer and his wife and children from much manual labor. With the very modern problem of agricultural surpluses in America, we forget that such food abundance is new and unique in human history.

It doesn't hurt to remind ourselves that in 1910, 25 percent of a farmer's land had to be used to raise feed for farm animals. One farmer produced enough food to feed 7.1 persons a year (I used to wonder about those .1 persons, but no longer; in my years in Washington, D.C., and in state and national politics, I've met plenty of them). Today one farmer feeds 59 people, instead of 7.1. In 1910, one farmer with a team of horses could plow one acre of land a day. Now, with tractors, he plows 35. In 1910, one acre yielded 26 bushels of corn, while today that same acre yields 97 bushels.

To produce today's crops without fuel and electricity and with 1910's technology would require 27 million more farm workers (there are only 4 million now) and 61 million more horses and mules. And it would take 20 years to breed the farm animals, since there are only three million now alive. How's that? Why not speed up the breeding? Because biology works by its own clock. With humans it takes nine months to make a baby. No matter what we tried—better nutrition, better doctors, spending more money, or mighty wishing—that time cannot be reduced. It still takes nine months. You can't even make nine women pregnant and get a baby in one month! It just won't work! Proposals to return to a pre-industrial type of agriculture are simply irresponsible.

Here we are, in the final decade of the twentieth century, a once buoyant nation with unbounded faith in the future and in our ability to make it better, but now so possessed by self-doubt and recrimination and so frightened that something might go wrong that we are unwilling to accept even minute amounts of personal or environmental risk. Too afraid to accept what is actually very good, we demand a guaranteed perfection, despite knowing that a 100 percent risk-free society is unobtainable.

In the modern world, there might be more important commodities than electrical energy, but it would be difficult to make such a case. Energy, particularly electricity, is the lifeblood of society. With electricity in sufficient amounts and at affordable cost from reliable and dependable sources, we can do anything, limited only by the technological genius that abounds in human minds.

It is worth repeating: Electricity is the cleanest, safest, cheapest, and most flexible form of energy yet known, but it is not perfect, and it is dangerous. Yet, it is so common and so useful that its ready availability at reasonable cost is considered a basic human right (at least that's the way state utility commissions consider it). But electricity is a commodity like any other; it is manufactured, distributed, and sold to all customers. Uniquely, a utility accepts a responsibility to provide service, cannot refuse to sell electricity (at least in the domestic retail market), and provides it *before* we pay.

It is strange how much a part of modern life electricity has become. Who remembers the fear, often bordering on hysteria, that accompanied its introduction? Who recalls that the world's most eminent body of scientists, the Royal Society of London, once met in special session to oppose its use? Declaring that Edison's ideas to electrify cities "defied scientific principle" and "wouldn't work," the Royal Society made a last-ditch effort to prevent electrification by adopting a resolution stating that electricity is "too powerful to put into the hands of common men." And who remembers the bitter feud between Thomas Edison and George Westinghouse as to whether alternating or direct current should be used?[4]

We are growing more and more dependent on electricity. In the steel industry, for example, electric arc furnaces now account for 37 percent of the American steelmaking capacity, an environmental blessing. Moreover, even though industrial use of *energy* grew only 1.1 percent between 1982 and 1986, industrial use of *electricity* grew by 8.5 percent. This was due mostly to greater use of automated processes and robotics. Electric power consumption, per unit produced, has increased by up to 50 percent in the automobile, oil, and fabric industries, by 20 to 30 percent in the chemical industries, and only slightly less in the plastic and paper industries.[5]

Whereas growth in overall energy use in the United States has slowed markedly since the oil embargo of 1973, growth in the use of electricity has risen 17 percent. Electricity sales rose 4.5 percent in 1987 and rose even faster in 1988.

But there is a problem. We have, on one hand, this factual record of growth, as well as the fact that economic growth parallels the use of electricity very closely. But on the other hand, utility and energy "experts" continue to forecast electricity load increases of only 1.5 to 2 percent. This may be partly because they felt burned when their forecasts for growth in the early to middle 1970s proved too optimistic. But it is also largely because government regulators and activist environmentalists have combined to make new construction for generating electricity virtually impossible. This could have important consequences.

The heat wave of the summer of 1988 and the bitter cold of the winter of 1988 and 1989 sent electricity use soaring in the Midwest, Northeast, and mid-Atlantic states. In the mid-Atlantic states, actual use was 6.6 percent higher than forecast and reductions in voltage, brownouts, and voluntary shutdowns (at the National Bureau of Standards and other public buildings) were common. Hospitals had to go on emergency diesel power to illuminate surgeries and, farther north, even New England's reliance on electricity imported from Canada was not enough to keep blackouts from closing Harvard University for the first time in its 300-year history.

While utilities plead with their customers to conserve and load management is widely practiced, the spectacle of utilities scrambling to buy power from outside their service area has become common.

In its recent assessment of the United States electric output,[6] the North American Electric Reliability Council (NERC) found in September 1988, that "utility plans will support an average annual growth in the demand for electricity of 2 percent in the United States." Although the NERC judged that two percent would be the most likely ten-year growth rate, it noted that there was a 50 percent chance the growth would be higher, (since 1979, electricity sales have grown by about four percent a year).

It wasn't the only qualification in the NERC report, nor was it the most troubling. The council came very close to conceding that its tally of new capacity planned for 1987–96 was suspect. Among the examples were these:

1. Construction has not yet started on almost 45 percent of the 90,000 megawatts of new generating capacity expected by 1996.

2. About 9,800 megawatts of the new capacity not yet under construction are coal-fired power stations with in-service dates that allow only five to nine years for construction. "Since it typically requires eight to ten years to license and build large coal units," the NERC wrote, "it seems likely that much of this new coal-fired capacity will either be completed late or replaced with shorter lead-time generator types."

3. Some 80 percent of the 2,500 megawatts of new hydroelectric capacity expected in the next nine years is not yet under construction.

4. Of the 17,300 megawatts of "other utility" generation expected on line by 1996, more than 90 percent is not being built.

5. Of the 11,500 megawatts of non-utility generation expected, nearly 85 percent is not yet under construction.

6. Construction has not yet started on nearly 20,000 miles of new high-voltage transmission lines. With many utilities planning to meet new demand by buying power from others, any delay in expanding transmission capacity is cause for concern. Bulk power sales now represent about 16 percent of all power sold in the United States and the amount of electricity wheeled in transmission agreements increased by 11 percent between 1976 and 1985.

An excess capacity of 15 to 20 percent is usually considered appropriate to take care of emergencies and outages. Remember, too, that much of the nation's generating equipment is aging and will require replacement within the next few years. The situation is not optimistic. Yet, utility managers cannot be faulted, since government regulators and activist environmentalists have combined to make new construction for generating electricity virtually impossible.

The decade of the 1990s should be one of significant expansion in the number of generating plants and their accompanying transmission lines. If new construction does not take place, the cost of electricity inevitably will rise.

Despite worrisome delays and restrictions on new construction, no one, including those most concerned with shortages, believes any region of the United States will ever be subject to blackouts. Two things will happen first, neither of them particularly pleasant.

First, economic growth will be lost in the areas in which electrical shortages are experienced. Manufacturers are not stupid. They will not expand capacity or build new manufacturing plants in areas facing problems with power supply. Industries contemplating expansion will simply move elsewhere. Industrial growth will be lost, as will the residential and commercial growth that would accompany industrial expansion.

Second, utilities will meet demand by building gas turbines, which can be installed fairly quickly and cheaply. The cost of electricity from these plants, fueled with oil or natural gas, will be high but the power will be necessary.

The Edison Electric Institute has acknowledged: "When we begin to get near the point where capacity is short, we are not making dire predictions about brownouts and blackouts. We are saying . . . we're likely to see some very uneconomic options selected to provide for power supply, which are not really in the long-term interest of our customers."

America may well end up having the highest-cost electricity among the industrialized nations. To say the least, this would not be a favorable factor in a competitive world.

Part Two

SAVING THE PLANET

Chapter 4

GREENHOUSE EARTH

THE YEAR 1988 ended on a high note of environmental hysteria about global warming, fueled by an unusually hot, dry summer (in the United States). Testifying at a Senate hearing, NASA's James Hansen claimed that the high temperatures presaged the onset of the long debated "greenhouse effect" caused by increased carbon dioxide (CO_2) in the atmosphere. [1]

Forgotten was the harsh winter of 1982, or of 1978, when, for example, barges carrying coal and heating oil froze in river ice and more than 200 people lost their lives in the cold weather.

Only days after *Time* magazine featured a doomed, overheated Earth as its "man of the year" for 1988, Alaska experienced the worst cold in its history. The freezing weather set in on January 12, 1989. Twenty different locations in our most northerly state recorded their lowest-ever temperatures, mainly in the range of −50 to −65 degrees Fahrenheit. At Tanana, near Fairbanks, −75 degrees Fahrenheit was reached. (The all-time low recorded anywhere in Alaska was −80 degrees in January 1971 at a Prospect Creek pipeline station.) The cold persisted; it did not moderate and begin to move south until the first week of February. Old-timers agreed that no such cold had ever been experienced before, and they expressed amazement that the temperature remained a chilly −16 degrees Fahrenheit along the coast even with an 81-knot wind blowing. This was unheard of, since usually it is coldest when the wind is quiet. In early February, the cold seeped down from Alaska along both sides of the Rocky Mountains, bringing near-record lows both to the Pacific Northwest and throughout the Midwest south to Texas and eventually to the mid-Atlantic and New England states. Proponents of the "greenhouse-is-here-global-warming-has-begun" theory were very quiet during these weeks.

To be fair, even if the projected greenhouse warming should occur, no one would expect it to happen all at once or without intervening cold spells. So let's examine the situation more closely.

Of course, the earth, with its enveloping blanket of atmosphere, constitutes a "greenhouse." This fact has never been at issue. Indeed, were it not for the greenhouse function of air, the earth's surface might be like the moon, bitterly cold (−270 degrees Fahrenheit) at night and unbearably hot (+212 degrees Fahrenheit) during the day. Although the amount of solar energy reaching the moon is essentially the same as that reaching earth, the earth's atmosphere acts like a filter. Of the incoming solar radiation, about 20 percent is absorbed in the atmosphere, about 50 percent reaches and warms the earth's surface, and the rest is reflected back into space. As the earth's surface is warmed up, infrared radiation is emitted. It is the presence of CO_2 (and water vapor, methane, hydrocarbon, and a few other gases) in the atmosphere that absorbs the long wavelength infrared radiation, thereby producing the warming "greenhouse effect." This accounts for a net warming of the earth's atmosphere system of about 55 degrees Fahrenheit. Without this natural greenhouse, it would be difficult to sustain life on this planet.

All the important "greenhouse gases" are produced in nature, as well as by humans. For example, CO_2 comes naturally from the respiration of all living organisms and from decaying vegetation. It is also injected into the atmosphere by volcanoes and forest and grass fires. Carbon dioxide from man-made sources comes primarily from burning fossil fuels for home and building heat, for transportation, and for industrial processes. The amount of CO_2 released into the atmosphere is huge and it is commonly believed that it is divided about evenly between natural and man-made sources.

Hydrocarbons come from growing plants, especially coniferous trees, such as fir and pine, and from various industries. In the transportation arena, hydrocarbons result from incomplete oxidation of gasoline. Both hydrocarbons and methane also enter the atmosphere through the metabolism of cows and other ruminants. It is estimated that American cows produce about 50 million tons of these gases per year—and there is no control technology for such emissions. Methane seeps into the air from swamps, coal mines, and rice paddies; it is often "flared" from oil wells. The largest source of greenhouse gas may well be termites, whose digestive activities are responsible for about 50 billion tons of CO_2 and methane annually. This is 10 times more than the present world production of CO_2 from burning fossil fuel. Methane may be oxidized in the atmosphere, leading to an estimated one billion tons of carbon monoxide per year. All in all, the atmosphere is a grand mixture of gases, in a constant state of turbulence, and yet maintained in an overall state of dynamic balance.

But now this balance appears to be disturbed as CO_2 and the other major greenhouse gases are on the rise, increasing their concentration in the air at a rate of about one percent per year. CO_2 is responsible for about half of the increase. Analysis of air bubbles trapped in glacial ice and of carbon isotopes in tree rings and ocean sediment cores indicate that CO_2 levels hovered around 260 to 280 parts per million from the end of the last ice age (10,000 years ago) till the mid-nineteenth century, except for an anomolous rise 300 years ago. And these measurements also show that CO_2 concentrations have varied widely (by 20 percent) as the earth has passed through glacial and interglacial periods. While today's 25 percent increase in CO_2 can be accounted for by the burning of fossil fuels, what caused the much greater increases in the prehistoric past?

The present increase has brought the CO_2 level to 340 parts per million, up about 70 parts per million. If we add the greater amounts of methane, hydrocarbons, and so forth, there is now a total of about 407 parts per million of greenhouse gases. This is large enough so that from the greenhouse effect alone we should have experienced a global warming of about two to four degrees Fahrenheit. But this has not happened.

The observed and recorded temperature pattern since 1880 does not fit with the CO_2 greenhouse warming calculations. During the 1880s, there was a period of cooling, followed by a warming trend. The temperature rose by one degree Fahrenheit during 1900 to 1940, then fell from 1940 to 1965, and then began to rise again, increasing by about 0.3 degrees Fahrenheit since 1975. When all these fluctuations are analyzed, it appears unlikely that there has been any overall warming in the last 50 years. And if the temperature measurements taken in the northern hemisphere are corrected for the urban effect—the so-called "heat island" that exists over cities due mainly to the altered albedo from removing vegetation—then it is probable that not only has there been no warming; there may have been a slight cooling. It all depends on whose computer model you choose to believe.

Clearly, there is still something that is not understood about global conditions and about the weather links between the oceans and the atmosphere. Have the experts fully taken into account the role of the sea as a sink or reservoir for CO_2, including the well known fact that much more CO_2 dissolves in cold water than in warm? Interest in the greenhouse gases and projections of global warming has stimulated greater interest in the role that the oceans play in influencing moderately or even drastically changing global climate. The oceans hold more CO_2 than does the atmosphere, 60 times more. Complex circulation patterns that involve waters of different temperature, together with the activities of marine organisms that deposit carbonate in their skeletons, carry carbon dioxide to the depths of the ocean.

Recall that all the public furor about global warming was triggered in June 1988, when NASA scientist James Hansen testified in the U.S. Senate that the greenhouse effect is changing the climate now! He said he was 99 percent sure of it, and that "1988 would be the warmest year on record, unless there is some remarkable, improbable cooling in the remainder of the year."[2] Well, there was. Almost while Dr. Hansen was testifying, the eastern tropical Pacific Ocean underwent a remarkable, improbable cooling—a sudden drop in temperature of seven degrees.

No one knows why. But the phenomenon is not unknown; it is called La Nina to distinguish it from the more commonly occurring El Nino, or warm current, and it has happened 19 times in the last 102 years.

Dr. Hansen did not consider the possibility of La Nina, because his computer program does not take sea temperatures into account. Yet the oceans cover 73 percent of the earth's surface.

When people, including scientists, talk "global," it is hard to believe that they can ignore 73 percent of the globe, but obviously they sometimes do. It is all the more astonishing to ignore ocean-atmosphere interactions, especially in the Pacific, when it is well established that El Nino has profound and widespread effects on weather patterns and temperatures; does it not follow that La Nina may also? Indeed, some atmospheric scientists credit the severely cold winter of 1988–89 to the earlier temperature drop in the tropical Pacific.

Once again, since the greenhouse gases are increasing, what's keeping the earth from warming up? There are a number of possible explanations. Perhaps there is some countervailing phenomenon that hasn't been taken into account; perhaps the oceans exert greater lag than expected and the warming is just postponed; perhaps the sea and its carbonate-depositing inhabitants are a much greater sink than some scientists believe; perhaps the increase in CO_2 stimulates more plant growth and removal of more CO_2 than calculated; perhaps there is some other greenhouse gas, like water vapor, that is more important than CO_2; perhaps varying cloud cover provides a greater feedback and self-correcting mechanism than has been taken into account; perhaps. . . . The fact is, there is simply not enough good data on most of these processes to know for sure what is happening in these enormous, turbulent, interlinked, dynamic systems like atmosphere and oceanic circulation. The only thing that can be stated with certainty is that they do affect the weather. So also do forces outside the planet, and in a moment we'll look at the sun in this regard.

First, we must acknowledge that some zealots in the greenhouse issue make much of deforestation, especially in the tropical rain forests, but this topic is marked more by emotion bordering on hysteria than on solid scientific data. Good measurements on CO_2 uptake and oxygen production in tropical rain forests are lacking. Such information could be critical, because we know that in temperate climates mature trees and climax forests add little in the way of photosynthetic activity and consequent CO_2 removal from the atmosphere. Mature trees, like all living things, metabolize more slowly as they grow old. A forest of young, vigorously growing trees will remove five to seven tons more CO_2 per acre per year than old growth.[3] There are plenty of good reasons to preserve old growth forests, but redressing the CO_2 balance is not one of them. If we are really interested (as we should be) in reducing atmospheric CO_2, we should be vigorously pursuing reforestation and the planting of trees and shrubs, including in urban areas, where local impacts on the atmosphere are greatest.

Reforestation *has* been going on through enlightened forestry practices on private lands by timber companies and as a result of changes in agriculture and land use. In the United States, the average annual wood growth is now more than three times what it was in 1920, and the growing stock has increased 18 percent from 1952 to 1977. Forests in America continue to increase in size, even while supplying a substantial fraction of the world's timber needs.[4]

Finally, it should be kept in mind that when a tree is cut for timber, it will no longer remove CO_2 from the atmosphere, but it won't release its stored carbon either—until or unless it is burned or totally decayed. In the whole deforestation question, it would be interesting to try to determine what effect the deforestation of Europe had on temperature and climate in the nineteenth century, and, similarly, what the effect was of the earlier deforestation of the Mediterranean area and the Middle East.

If we study history, we find that there is no good or widely accepted explanation for why the earth's temperature and climate were as they were at any particular time in the past, including the recurring ice ages and the intervening warm periods. What caused the "little ice age" of the late seventeenth century and why was it preceded by 800 years of relative warmth? Is all this really due to human activity? What about natural phenomena? Recent studies of major deep sea currents in the Atlantic ocean suggest a causative relation to the onset of ice ages.[5]

Occasional unusual actions by nature can release great quantities of CO_2 and other greenhouse gases to the atmosphere.

I received my lesson in humility, my respect for the size and vast power of natural forces on May 18, 1980. For those who might not instantly recognize that date, it was a Sunday, a beautiful spring morning when at 8:31 Mount St. Helens erupted with the force of more than 500 atomic bombs. Gases and particulate matter were propelled 80,000 feet, approximately 15 miles, into the stratosphere and deposited above the ozone layer. The eruption continued for nearly 12 hours and more than four billion tons of earth were displaced.[6]

Because Mount St. Helens is relatively accessible, there were many studies conducted and good data are available on the emissions—at least those that occurred after May 18. For the remaining seven months of 1980, Mount St. Helens released 910,000 metric tons of CO_2, 220,000 metric tons of sulfur dioxide, and unknown amounts of aerosols into the atmosphere. Many other gases, including methane, water vapor, carbon monoxide, and a variety of sulfur compounds were also released, and emissions still continue to seep from the crater and from fumaroles and crevices.

Gigantic as it was, Mount St. Helens was not a large volcanic eruption. It was dwarfed by Mount St. Augustine and Mount Redoubt in Alaska in 1976 and 1989 and El Chicon in Mexico in 1982. El Chicon was an exceptionally sulfurous eruption. The violence of its explosion sent more than 100 million tons of sulfur gases high into the stratosphere. Droplets of sulfuric acid formed; these continue to rain down onto the earth's surface. The earth, at present, appears to be in a period of active volcanism, with volcanic eruptions occurring at a rate of about 100 per year. Most of these are in remote locations, where accurate measurement of the gaseous emissions is not possible, but they must be considerable. Some estimates from large volcanic eruptions in the past suggest that all of the air polluting materials produced by man since the beginning of the industrial revolution do not begin to equal the quantities of toxic materials, aerosols, and particulates spewed into the air from just three volcanoes: Krakatoa in Indonesia in

1883, Mount Katmai in Alaska in 1912, and Hekla in Iceland in 1947.[7] Despite these prodigious emissions, Krakatoa, for example, produced some chilly winters, spectacular sunsets, and a global temperature drop of 0.3 degrees Centigrade, but no climate change. From written records, we also know that the famous "year without a summer" that followed the eruption of Mount Tambora in 1816 meant that the summer temperature in Hartford, Connecticut, did not exceed 82 degrees Fahrenheit. No doom.

We can conclude from these volcanic events that the atmosphere is enormous and its capacity to absorb and dilute pollutants is also very great. This is no excuse, of course, to pollute the air deliberately, which would be an act of folly. But it does give us some perspective on events.

So far, we have considered only those phenomena that occur on earth that might influence global temperature, weather, and eventually the climate. "Weather" means the relatively short-term fluctuations in temperature, precipitation, winds, cloudiness, and so forth, that shift and change over periods of hours, days, or weeks. Weather patterns may be cyclic, more or less repeating themselves every few years. The "climate," on the other hand, is generally accepted to be the mean of weather changes over a period of about 30 years. Weather may change rapidly, but the climate may remain essentially the same over thousands of years, as it probably has for the last 8,000 years.

Now, what about the effects on weather of extraterrestrial phenomena? After all, it is the sun that determines the climate on earth—but the role of the sun, with its ever-shifting solar radiation, is generally ignored as being inconsequential in affecting shorter-term weather patterns. But is this really so?

Consider: the earth shifts in its position relative to the sun. Its orbit is eccentric, varying over a period of 97,000 years. The inclination of the earth's axis shifts with respect to the ecliptic over a cycle of 41,000 years, and the precession of the equinox varies over a period of 21,000 years. How do these shifts affect the amount of solar radiation reaching the earth? Some astronomers believe that at least for the last 500,000 to one million years, these phenomena are related to the initiation and dissipation of glacial and interglacial intervals.

Although it may seem to us that the sun is stable and stationary, it is in fact whirling through the Milky Way galaxy, taking its family of planets with it. Activity on the sun itself goes through periods of relative quiet and then erupts into flares and protuberances, sunspots, and gigantic upheavals that "rain" solar material out into space.[8] One recent solar storm was measured at 43,000 miles across. This produced the largest solar flare ever recorded. Some of the increased solar radiation from such storms reaches the earth and disrupts radio communication and television transmission and increases the aurora borealis.[9] Solar activity in the form of storms seen as sunspots has a span of roughly 11 years. It seems that the sunspots whirl clockwise for about 11 years, then reverse and go counterclockwise for another 11 years. This interval is an average and may vary from 7 to 17 years. The controlling mechanism for this reversal is unknown.

Then there is another variable. The sun "flickers"; that is, it dims and brightens slightly over a period of about 70 years. When it dims, the sunspots attain lower maxima. When the sun brightens, the sunspots have higher maxima than "normal." Although this dimming and brightening has been suspected for some time, the first actual measurement of such a "flicker" was made on April 4, 1980, when a satellite measuring solar radiation outside the earth's atmosphere recorded a 0.2 percent drop in radiation. Changes in solar radiation are now routinely measured.

Coupled with the activity of the sun, there is the moon's gravitational force, to which the earth's waters respond daily and in 28-day cycles of tides. Also, there are 20-year and 60-year tidal cycles, as well as longer ones. Moreover, the solid land also responds to the moon's gravitational force, but because we move with the ground, we do not feel it. Recently, a 556-year variation in the moon's orbit around the earth was analyzed; some meteorologists believe that the occasional confluence of all these sun-and-moon cycles may trigger dramatic changes in ocean currents and temperatures. And it is now widely acknowledged that the oceans are a major influence on the climate. There is also a 500-to-600-year cycle in volcanic activity, which appears to be near a peak at the present time.

Let's consider again. Does all this variability in solar activity really have anything to do with weather or climate? No one knows for certain. But studies are continuing, and Dr. John Eddy of the National Center for Atmospheric Research has found an interesting correlation between decades of low sunspot activity and cold periods, such as the "little ice age" of the seventeenth century, when there was a virtual absence of sunspot activity between 1645 and 1715, and decades of high sunspot activity with warm temperatures on earth.[10]

Since the sunspot cycle is not perfectly regular and varies considerably, how do scientists determine the extent of sunspot activity that occurred decades or centuries ago? This is a neat piece of scientific detective work that merits a brief explanation. It involves another extraterrestrial phenomenon—cosmic radiation.

Cosmic rays consist of high energy particles that enter the earth's atmosphere from outer space. These energetic particles split the nuclei of atmospheric gases, giving rise to some of the background radiation to which all living organisms are exposed. Among the fission products are Potassium-40 and Carbon-14, which get into the food chain and are eaten (by animals) or absorbed (by plants), and that is one of the reasons that the bodies of all living organisms are radioactive. Of these two fission products, it is Carbon-14 that is the most interesting for tracing events in the past.

C-14, whose half-life is a relatively short 5,570 years, is being produced continuously in the atmosphere (through interaction with cosmic rays) and is continuously taken up by *living* organisms, but not by dead ones. Therefore, by measuring the amount of C-14 in dead or fossil material, one can infer the date of death. This is called carbon-dating. C-14 is a very good but not perfect clock of history, because the assumption is that the formation of C-14 is not only continuous but also that it occurs at a steady rate. But what Dr. Eddy has determined is that the rate of formation varies with the amount of cosmic radiation, which, in turn, varies with the amount of sunspot activity, because high solar activity also creates more solar wind that can compress the earth's magnetic field. This stronger field is more effective in shielding cosmic rays from the earth's atmosphere, which means that less C-14 is formed during periods of high sunspot activity. Less C-14 equates with warmer periods on earth.

Taking advantage of these phenomena, Dr. Eddy measured the C-14 radioactivity in tree rings in trees that are up to 5,000 years old. Keep in mind that the years (rings) of low C-14 equate with years of high solar activity and warm temperatures. Dr. Eddy recorded 12 prolonged periods with either unusually cold or unusually mild winters over the last 5,000 years. These correlations between solar activity and weather on earth seem good; his measurements identified the terrible winter of 1683–84, also recorded in the novel *Lorna Doone*, when trees in Somerset, England, froze and many exploded from the buildup of internal ice.

If Dr. Eddy's work and theory hold up, the mid-twentieth century was an unusually warm period, and the earth may be set soon to enter a slow return to cooler temperatures. Besides, in geologically recent times, ice ages recur about every 11,000 to 12,000 years, and it is now 11,000 years since the last one. How do all these complications interact with the greenhouse effect? Again, no one really knows. All we can say with confidence is that it is probably more complicated than many environmentalists seem to believe. [11]

When we consider all of the complex geophysical phenomena that might affect the weather and climate on earth, from changes in ocean temperatures and currents, volcanic eruptions, solar storms, and cyclic movements of heavenly bodies, it is clear that none of these is under human control or could be influenced by human activity. Is the "greenhouse effect" and its theoretical enhancement by increases in atmospheric CO_2 from human sources more powerful or capable of overshadowing all other planetary influences? Until the supporters of the man-produced-CO_2-caused-global-warming-theory can explain warm and cold episodes in the past, we should remain skeptical. [12] What caused the 80 parts per million increase in CO_2 during a 100-year period 300 years ago and the high peak—many times anything measured since—of 130,000 years ago?

The alteration of the chemical content of the air by *human* production of greenhouse gases, however, is something that man *can* control. And because no one knows what the ultimate consequences of heightened CO_2 might be, it is reasonable and responsible to reduce human contribution wherever possible.

Fortunately, there are ways to accomplish this. For starters, we can phase out the use of fossil fuel for making electricity and turn to the established and proven technology that has no adverse impact on the atmosphere—nuclear power. The energy of the atom now produces 20 percent of the electricity in the United States—more than the total of all electricity used in 1950. The number of nuclear power plants can be increased. [13]

Second, we can shift to an essentially all-electric economy, utilizing electricity for direct heating of buildings and homes and extending the use of electric processes in industry. With enough electricity available, it can also be used to desalinate sea water and purify the fresh water sources that have become polluted. It can also be used to split water and obtain hydrogen, which has great potential as a clean fuel for transportation. Its "burning" produces only water vapor.

And we can turn, once again, to electric buses and trains, and eventually to electric automobiles.

None of these shifts away from fossil fuels will be easy or fast, but if we have an abundance of electricity from nuclear power plants, it can be done. That would leave fossil fuels for the important synthetics and plastics industries, and for the manufacture of medicinals, pesticides, and fertilizers.

There are also two important caveats; though steps to reduce CO_2 production may be possible for an advanced, highly technical, industrialized society with plenty of electricity, the infrastructure to make use of it, and money to spend, the story is different in the non-industrialized world. In China, for example, 936 million metric tons of coal were burned in 1987. Who is going to tell China to stop or to change? What alternative do the Chinese have? No matter what we in the Western world do, the amount of CO_2 arising from human use of fossil fuel will not be significantly reduced. [14]

The second caveat is to remember that draconian measures intended to make rapid and large decreases in CO_2 formation won't do much good if they are so costly that they seriously impede the economy and degrade our standard of living without achieving the desired result. Certainly the level of atmospheric CO_2 is increasing, but nothing in all our knowledge of weather and climate guarantees that global warming will inevitably occur. It may, or it may not; the uncertainties are legion. The computer models are too simplistic and include too many estimates and guesses and too little about the role of the hydrosphere, both water vapor and the oceans. [15]

Notwithstanding all this, deliberate, reasoned steps can and should be taken to lower CO_2 emissions; responsible stewardship of the planet demands no less.

Finally, let's suppose that a worst case scenario does develop and that global warming does occur. If the warming caused polar ice to melt, only that on land, as in the Antarctic continent (or the glaciers of Greenland), would materially affect global sea level. When ice floats, as in the Arctic ocean, it already displaces approximately the same amount of water that would result if it were to melt. (There would be some slight thermal expansion.) Whether Arctic ice stays solid or melts would no more cause the sea level to rise than ice cubes melting would cause a full glass of ice water to overflow.

Analysis of sea level data since 1900 indicates that the oceans may be rising at a rate of 10 to 25 centimeters per century (about 0.1 inch per year). The data are very sketchy and uncertain. The sea rise, if it is real, is not uniform and other phenomena, such as land subsidence or upthrust, the building and erosion of beaches by weather, and the variation of inshore currents, could all affect the few measurements that are available.

Some scientists postulate that the west Antarctic ice sheet, which is anchored on bedrock below sea level, could melt and add enough water to raise the world sea level by six or seven meters. This would be disastrous for most coastlines, but if it should happen, it would probably take several hundred years, and there is currently neither observational evidence nor scientific measurements to indicate that it is under way. In fact, new measurements show that the glaciers in Antarctica are growing, not melting. [16]

Air temperatures in Antarctica average −40 degrees Centigrade. A five-degree rise in air temperature to −35 degrees Centigrade is certainly not enough to melt ice. But somewhat warmer sea water (above one degree Centigrade) might get under the ice sheet and start it slipping into the sea; then it would float and displace an enormous volume of water, causing the sea level to rise. But this is also a very unlikely "what if?" with no evidence to support it.

Now, what about ozone in the stratosphere; how significant are the "holes" measured above Antarctica? Are we humans destroying our protective cover? Quite a few people seem to think so.

But let me start with a quotation from an analysis of the ozone problem published in the 1987–88 Annual Report of the Rand Corporation:[17]

> The extent of ozone depletion and the severity of the consequences of projected emission levels are extremely uncertain. Projections of future depletion are based on complex simulation models that have not been reconciled with the limited available measurements. . . .
>
> Because of pervasive uncertainty about the likely extent of future ozone depletion, its relationship to the quantity of potential ozone depleters emitted, its effect on the biosphere, and the appropriate valuation of these consequences, it is not currently possible to choose the level of emission-limiting regulations that will maximize welfare by optimally balancing costs of environmental damage against those of emission control. Policymakers must act in the face of this uncertainty.

Is that all perfectly clear? What the writer is trying to say, diplomatically, I think, is that nobody knows how much ozone depletion has really taken place or what effect, if any, that ozone loss may have on the environment or on living creatures. The Rand Corporation writer emphasizes that present knowledge of ozone layer thickness is full of uncertainty and that the conclusions that have been drawn are based on incomplete computer models. There is little reliable, accurate, direct measurement. Nevertheless, he says, "policymakers must act. . . ." Why? Because some doom-predicting scientists say that "irreversible damage may occur"? What is their evidence?

Given the media hoopla and hysteria surrounding the ozone issue, surely it is time to examine the whole question with some sober common sense.

We know that the earth's ozone layer is turbulent. It undergoes periodic changes in thickness. Natural fluctuations are about 15 percent and it quickly returns to equilibrium. Changes appear to be both seasonal and latitudinal. Seasonal changes above Antarctica are largest when measured at the end of winter. The changes in ozone layer thickness in Antarctica have now been measured in the Arctic, as well. (No one looked until recently.)

The best measurement data indicate that the ozone layer increased in average thickness during the 1960s and decreased during 1979–86. The decreases were comparable in magnitude to the increases of the 1960s.

The term, ozone "hole," is misleading, since it persists for only a few weeks. The Antarctic ozone "hole" grew during the early 1980s, becoming large in 1985, smaller in 1986, and reaching its greatest size in 1987. In 1988, the "hole" did not appear as expected. It was finally discovered—only 15 percent as large as predicted and displaced over the ocean.

The changes in the amount of ozone appear to be related to complex chloride chemistry and the presence of nitrous oxide. Although there is widespread belief that the necessary chloride ion comes from chlorofluorocarbon (CFC) this has not been unequivocally established. On the other hand, the eruption of Mount St. Augustine (Alaska) in 1976 injected 289 billion kilograms of hydrochloric acid directly into the stratosphere. That amount is 570 times the total world production of chlorine and fluorocarbon compounds in the year 1975. Mount Erebus, which is located just 15 kilometers upwind from McMurdo Sound, has been erupting, constantly, for the last 100 years, ejecting more than 1,000 tons of chlorine per day. Since the world production of CFC peaked at 1.1 million tons per year—equivalent to 750,000 tons of chlorine, and 300 million tons of chlorine reach the atmosphere each year through evaporation of sea water alone—we cannot be sure where the stratospheric chloride comes from, and whether humans have any effect upon it.

So much is known.[18] Most atmospheric scientists also agree that ozone molecules are being created and destroyed naturally by very short wavelengths of ultraviolet light from the sun. Since the same narrow band of ultraviolet light that breaks down chlorofluorocarbons (CFCs) to destroy ozone also breaks down oxygen to create ozone, the result is a balance between these two processes, a competition between CFC and O_2 for the necessary solar energy. Moreover, the result depends on the relative abundance of the two gases (CFC and O_2) in the ozone layer, and data from the National Oceanic and Atmospheric Administration (NOAA) show 60,000 ozone molecules created for every one destroyed by chlorine from a CFC molecule. It is quite possible that overall depletion of ozone is *not* occurring and indeed the NOAA data from measurements taken at the surface of the earth indicate that the total amount of ozone above the United States is actually increasing. In addition, it is known that interaction of solar wind with the earth's magnetic field, which causes the auroras, can also destroy stratospheric ozone. Solar wind comes from solar flares and these are increasing in the present period of sunspot maxima.

So is the sky falling? Still being debated among atmospheric scientists is whether the recently measured ozone changes have been occurring all along or whether they are a new phenomenon sparked by human activity or perhaps a combination of both. To quote a January 1989 summary published in *Science* (Vol. 239), "the recent losses may be natural and may result from long-term fluctuations of the general circulation of the atmosphere." Some researchers, pointing out that atmospheric dynamics can cause big changes in ozone, describe a 48-hour period at the beginning of September 1988, when the ozone decreased 10 percent over a 3 million square kilometer area. Robert T. Watson, head of NASA's upper atmospheric research program, said, "In our opinion, all provisional, we do not believe that change can be chemical [that is, caused by CFCs]. It is strong evidence that *meteorological processes alone* can effectively depress areas of ozone over the Antarctic continent." Direct evidence has yet to be produced, and Robert Watson of NASA reported that the optical diffuser plate on the Nimbus satellite had deteriorated so rapidly in space that its ozone depletion measurements are "useless garbage."

Against this background of uncertainty and the conviction of some respected scientists that natural processes may account for ozone "holes," how can public officials and governmental representatives seriously consider taking drastic action—for example, to ban CFCs—as if that would "cure" the problem, if indeed there is a problem?

Consider that in the United States economy alone, CFCs, mainly freon, are used in 100 million refrigerators, 90 million cars and trucks, 40,000 supermarket display cases, and 100,000 building air conditioners. It is estimated that banning CFCs would mean changing or replacing capital equipment valued at $135 billion. And all the proposed substitutes have problems; none is in production, most of them are toxic, and many are flammable. Of course, we could always return to using toxic ammonia and sulfur dioxide! Note that one of the biggest users of freon is refrigeration, and the most important reason for refrigeration is food preservation. If the proponents of banning CFC are so anxious to reduce its use, why aren't they out campaigning for irradiating food as a substitute for refrigeration? Food irradiation is an available technology used by all our astronauts and in hospitals for patients that require a sterile environment.

We are told that the ozone hole is important because the ozone blanket blocks much of the ultraviolet light in sunshine, which, if it penetrates to the earth's surface, could cause skin cancer, eye problems, and plant damage. This could be worrisome, except that actual records from a network of recording instruments set up in 1974 to measure ultraviolet light reaching the earth's surface have shown a continuously decreasing penetration of from 0.5 percent to 1.1 percent per year. If the theories about ozone depletion were correct, ultraviolet radiation should have been increasing, not decreasing.[19]

Furthermore, the form of skin cancer caused by ultraviolet radiation is relatively harmless, though irritating and unsightly, and 99 percent of the cases can be cured if treated in time. On the other hand, malignant melanoma, another unrelated type of skin cancer, is generally fatal. Its appearance is not related to ultraviolet radiation; its cause is unknown. Tragically, it is increasing, by 800 percent since 1935. As for plants, most are protected by several mechanisms that function to repair damage caused by ultraviolet light. The conclusion is hard to avoid: that the claims of skin cancer due to ozone loss are simply a widely repeated scare tactic.

The historian Hans Morgenthau wrote in 1946:

> Two moods determine the attitude of our civilization to the social world: confidence in the power of reason, as represented by modern science, to solve the social problems of the age, and despair at the ever renewed failure of scientific reason to solve them.
>
> The intellectual and moral history of mankind is the story of inner insecurity, of the anticipation of impending doom, of metaphysical anxieties.

John Maddox, editor of the prestigious British journal *Nature* has said that "these days there also seems to be an underlying cataclysmic sense among people. Scientists don't seem to be immune to this."

Well, they ought to be. And we ought to remember that using our technology will go a long way toward averting those cataclysmic events and the "doom-is-almost-here" philosophy that seems to have so much appeal. Scientists owe it to society to show the way to a better life and an improved environment—through quality technology.

Chapter 5

ACID RAIN

A N ACID RAIN DEBATE has been going on for more than a decade. Public concern in the United States probably dates from a widely publicized 1974 report that concluded "the Northeastern U.S. has an extensive and severe acid precipitation problem." Does it? Probably. Is rain actually acidic? Yes. Does acid rain, or, preferably, acid precipitation, really damage forests, lakes, streams, fish, buildings, and monuments? Yes, in some instances, but not as the primary or only cause.

Can the adverse environmental effects that have been attributed to acid rain, whatever the real cause, be mitigated by reducing the amount of sulfur dioxide emitted to the atmosphere from industrial sources? No. What evidence there is suggests that it will not make much difference. Is enough known and understood about acid precipitation to warrant spending billions in public funds on supposed corrective measures? Certainly not.

Clearly, the U.S. Environmental Protection Agency has agreed with this assessment, for the agency's former administrator, Lee M. Thomas, said in 1986: "Current scientific data suggest that environmental damage would not worsen materially if acidic emissions continued at their present levels for 10 or 20 more years. Acid rain is a serious problem, but it is not an emergency."[1]

That rain is acidic has been known for a long time. Among the first records are a reference to acid rain in Sweden in 1848 and a discussion of English rain in 1872. Sulfur dioxide was established as a possible cause of damage to trees and other plants in Germany in 1867. The commonly repeated alarm that rainfall has become increasingly acidic over the last 25 years rests for its validity on an influential and frequently cited series of articles by G. E. Likens and his co-workers published in the 1970s.[2]

Careful evaluation by a group of scientists at Environmental Research and Technology, Inc., reveals that Likens's research suffered from problems in data collection and analysis, errors in calculations, questionable averaging of some data, selection of results to support the desired conclusions, and failure to consider all the available data. In a more recent critique,[3] similar conclusions were reached. Besides analyzing Likens's methods of determining rain acidity, Vaclav Smil examined maps of the distribution of acid precipitation in the eastern United States between the mid-1950s and the mid-1960s, which had been prepared by Likens *et al* and publicized as providing "unassailable proofs" of rising acidity.

"In reality," Smil concludes, "the measurement errors, incompatibility of collection and analytical procedures, inappropriate extrapolations, weather effects, and local interferences make such maps very dubious."

How could such flawed investigations be accepted? As Smil aptly remarked, "The history of science is replete with episodes where cases of dubious veracity were publicized as irreproachable truths. . . . It may be irrational, but even in science, those who make the first and often sensational claim get much wider attention and are credited with more credibility than those who come later with calm facts."

It is an unfortunate human trait to prefer to believe the worst, especially in environmental matters. We really do like to be scared. We like to blame someone, to make sure that someone "pays." No one understands this better than those who call themselves "environmentalists." And so, when a public alarm is raised, whether the issue is pesticides, bioengineering, toxic waste, nuclear power, or whatever, plenty of spokesmen for so-called environmental organizations repeat the alarms over and over. Accusations of harm or wrongdoing, whether supported by reliable data or not, tend to carry great authority. The followup sober analysis and careful evaluation of data by scientists is frequently ignored or drowned out by the activist environmentalists, who shout "Coverup!" and "Whitewash!" So it is with acid rain.

To make an objective evaluation of the claims and counterclaims in this fractious topic of the acidity of rainwater, we should start with a brief, if somewhat superficial, look at water and rainwater itself.

About Water

For a substance as necessary and as commonplace as water is, this unique material is surprisingly misunderstood and unappreciated. Everyone knows that water is essential for life; everyone expects it to be cheap, pure, and readily available. Few realize that of all the planets in our solar system, only Earth has large quantities of water in all of its phases—water vapor, liquid water, and ice. Water is one of only a very small number of substances found on Earth as a gas, liquid, and solid, all within the temperature range normally prevailing in nature.

Few realize, too, that you can't "use water up." There is just as much water now, no more and no less, than when it was first formed, eons ago. This is because water moves in a continuous cycle, evaporating from the surface of the oceans and to a lesser extent from the land and from the bodies of plants (transpiration) and animals (sweating, panting), condenses into clouds, and precipitates as rain. A single inch of rainfall on a single acre (one acre inch) means that 113 tons of water had first to be lifted to heights of 20,000 feet.

The average annual rainfall on earth, which is the same as the average annual evaporation, is about 30 inches; this is equivalent to more than 100 million billion gallons. Of course, rain does not fall uniformly; hence, in some localities at some times, rainfall exceeds evaporation and in other regions at other times, the reverse is true.

Over all, the pattern of excess precipitation and drought is made up by circulation of the oceans and the atmosphere so that the total amount of rainfall remains about the same worldwide, and sea level is relatively unchanged, while patterns of flood and drought constantly recur.

Rain forms when molecules of water vapor condense on ice crystals or salt crystals or minute particles of dust in clouds and then coalesce to form droplets that respond to the force of gravity. As rain falls through the atmosphere, it can "pick up" or "wash out" chemicals or other foreign materials or pollutants that may be present. Because water is such a good solvent, even in the cleanest air, rainwater dissolves some of the naturally present carbon dioxide, forming carbonic acid. Hence, rainwater is *always acidic*, or, if you like, acid rain is normal. There is no such thing as naturally neutral rainwater. Scientific studies generally distinguish between "acid rain"—that is, the acidity of rainwater itself—and "acid deposition"—the fallout of sulfates, nitrates, and other acidic substances. Acid deposition may be "wet" if washed out of the atmosphere with rain, or it may be "dry" if gases or particles simply settle out.

How acidic is pure water? Despite the fact that water molecules are very stable, with a chemical composition of two parts hydrogen to one part oxygen (H_2O), the molecular structure or architecture is somewhat asymmetrical. The molecules tend both to clump and to dissociate in response to inter-molecular forces. Dissociation leads to a few hydrogen ions carrying a positive charge—acidity—and an equal number of OH, or hydroxyl ions, with a negative charge—alkalinity.

Under normal conditions, in pure distilled water, only a few molecules are dissociated—in fact, about two ten-millionths of one percent. Now that's an awkward numerical expression. Therefore, for greater ease in expressing the number of dissociated molecules, which is the measure of relative acidity, a method called pH has been adopted. The pH of pure water is 7, the numerical expression of neutrality. Any pH measure below 7 is acidic, and any above 7 is basic or alkaline. The pH scale is logarithmic, like the Richter scale for measuring the intensity of earthquakes. Therefore, a change of one pH unit, from pH 5 to pH 6, is a tenfold change.

Water in the atmosphere normally contains some carbonic acid from dissolved carbon dioxide, and the pH of clean rainwater, even in pristine regions of the earth, is about pH 5.0 to 5.5. To simplify it, let me put it this way: The pH of clean rainwater compares to that of carrots, which are pH 5.0, and it lies between the acidity of spinach, pH 5.4, and bananas, which are pH 4.6. To offer another example, rainwater is far less acidic than cola drinks at pH 2.2.

Any lower pH than 5.0 is believed to be environmentally damaging. Lakes, streams, rivers, ponds, indeed all bodies of fresh water may and usually do receive dissolved material, either acidic or alkaline, from runoff and from the soil or the earthen basin over which the water stands or flows. Both acid and alkaline lakes are natural phenomena, and they exist without intervention by humans.

Getting an accurate measure of the pH of rainwater is more difficult than it may seem at first. Certainly it is no simple litmus test. Accurate procedures require careful laboratory analysis. For example, early work—that is, measurements taken before 1968—generally used soft glass containers. It is now known that even when the containers were carefully cleaned and when the analysis was done very soon after collection, the soft glass contributed alkalinity to the sample. And this increased with time in storage. Indeed, the range of error attributable to the use of soft glass is sufficient so that it might account for the difference in pH measurements between 1955–56 and 1965–66 reported by Coghill and Likens. Rainwater collection made in metal gauges, a common procedure before the 1960s, also influenced the results. An experiment to test this difference, using a diluted solution of sulfuric acid with a pH of 4.39, gave a reading of pH 5.9 when held for a short time in a metal gauge.

It is also now known that a rainwater sample taken at the beginning of a storm will give a pH reading different from that taken during and at the end of the rainfall. And it is also now known that measurements may differ widely at different locales within a region and that weather and climate affect the results. With regard to this last phenomenon, it may be that the more alkaline results reported by Coghill and Likens for the northeastern United States in the 1950s were related to the drought conditions that prevailed during those years. By contrast, the 1960s were rainy. When dry conditions persist, dust particles are more prevalent, and if they are present in the rain samples, they can neutralize some of the acidity and shift the pH toward the alkaline end of the scale.

For several reasons, then, it now appears that the historical data on which so much of the alarm and worry has been based, are of insufficient quality and quantity to establish as indisputable a trend toward higher acidity in the rainfall of the northeastern United States.

Complicating the acid rain picture still further are results of samples recently collected from ice frozen in the geological past, and from rainfall in remote regions of the earth. These results suggest that the relationship between acidity and the industrial production of sulfur dioxide emissions is at best extremely tenuous.

Analysis of icepack samples in the Antarctic and in the Himalayas indicates that precipitation deposited at intervals hundreds and thousands of years ago in those pristine environments had a pH value of 4.4 to 4.8. Some measurements were as low as 4.2. Examination of Greenland icepack samples shows that many times in the last 7,000 years, the acidity of rain was as high as pH 4.4.[4] In some cases, the periods of extremely high acidity lasted for a year or more. Coal burning utilities spewing out sulfur dioxide could not have been responsible, but these periods of high acidity do correspond to times of major volcanic eruptions. Also remarkable is the period of low acidity in the ice lasting from 1920 to 1960, when no major volcanic eruptions occurred but industrial pollution increased.

Recent measurements taken by the National Oceanic and Atmospheric Administration on Mauna Loa in Hawaii at 3,500 meters above sea level gave average pH values of 4.9, regardless of wind direction. Moreover, sampling at Cape Matatula on American Samoa, a monitoring site selected for its extreme cleanliness, resulted in measurements from pH 4.5 to 6.0 in the rainwater.

To gather more systematic data on the pH of rain in remote areas, a Global Precipitation Chemistry Project was set up in 1979. Samples of rainwater were tested from five sites—Northern Australia, Southern Venezuela, Central Alaska, Bermuda, and Amsterdam Island in the Southern Indian Ocean, halfway between Africa and Australia. The first results were published in 1982. Precipitation everywhere was acidic, pH values averaging between 4.8 and 5.0. I suppose it's possible to imagine that the Bermuda results could have been affected by long range transport of sulfate aerosols or other atmospheric pollution from the United States, or that the Alaskan atmosphere is polluted from coal burning in the Midwest. But that doesn't appear to be reasonable. At the remaining sites, including American Samoa, it's clear that man-made emissions could not have caused the measured acidity.

Conversely, in some areas where one might expect a low pH, actual measurements of the rainwater reveal higher than anticipated pH values. Twelve sites in Mexico, for example, measured pH 6.2 to 6.8. Nine inland sites in India gave a median pH of 7.5, with a range of 5.8 to 8.9. It turns out that the expected natural acidity of the rain is neutralized by suspended alkaline particles, mainly dust from dry fields, unpaved streets, and so on.

In China, 70 percent of the basic energy comes from burning coal. Sulfur dioxide releases are very high, particularly in urban areas. Nevertheless, rainwater in Peking is close to neutral, most values falling between pH 6.0 and 7.0. Interestingly, the same samples have heavy concentrations of sulfate and nitrate ions, as well as suspended alkaline matter, probably dust blown from desert regions. The pH is determined by complex interaction among these aerosols, ions, and particles.

Acid rain can also be buffered or neutralized by soil conditions. Recent studies at nearly 200 sites in the U.S. show that in the Northern Great Plains, high levels of calcium and magnesium ions occur, along with ammonia associated with animal husbandry and fertilizers. These combine to neutralize acidic precipitation. In the western half of North America, 75 to 96 percent of all acid anions—which are negatively charged ions—are so neutralized.

By way of contrast, in the northeastern United States, 52 percent of all acid anions are not so neutralized. [5] It might be that lower levels of alkaline dust, especially in the Northeast, are a consequence of successful air pollution control, resulting in the effective capture of particulate matter from industrial smoke. This possibility was investigated by Smil in 1985. He reported a great loss of airborne alkaline material between the mid-1950s and mid-1960s. Although exact and accurate calculations are not possible, reasonable estimates are that the annual production of largely alkaline particulate emissions fell by more than half between the 1950s and 1975. This loss resulted from large-scale replacement of coal as fuel for homes, transportation, and industrial boilers; highly efficient removal of fly ash from flue gases and tough emission controls on the iron, steel, and cement industries; as well as the covering of barren, dusty land with settlements, paved roads, lawns, and considerable regrowth of forests.

Another contributing factor to loss of alkaline materials may have been the practice of prompt extinction of forest fires. Wildfires, when left to burn themselves out, result in an accumulation of alkaline ash, which, together with the minerals it contains, acts to buffer natural acidity in the soil and redress the mineral imbalance.

One final point should be made about natural acidity and alkalinity. Soils along the North Pacific Coast tend to be quite acidic, a usual feature in areas that had been glaciated. Peat bogs are common. Cranberries, huckleberries, blueberries, and Douglas Fir trees, all requiring acid soil, are abundant. For comparison, soils in the arid West and Southwest are alkaline, and rarely measure a pH below 9.0. By contrast, the soils in New England are among the most acid in the world. Representative Adirondack soil measures pH 3.4. Soils in southeastern Canada are similar. That region also was glaciated, and the thin, poor soil overlays acid granitic material. In other words, the soils of the northeastern United States are by nature acidic, and always have been, environmentalist claims notwithstanding.

There is an extensive and growing body of scientific literature on atmospheric chemistry, much of it highly technical.[6] Gradually, understanding is also growing, but many areas of uncertainty remain. Experts are divided on exactly how acids are formed in clouds, in rainwater, and upon deposition. There is some disagreement, too, on the relative amount and importance of acid precursors from manmade versus natural sources. Most knowledgeable scientists tend to take a middle view—that the amount of pollutants in the air, particularly of sulfates and nitrates, on a global scale comes about equally from natural and human sources. But even this is a supposition or educated guess.

Natural Sources

Sulfur and nitrogen compounds—the "acid" in acid rain—are produced naturally by the decay of organic matter in swamps, wetlands, intertidal areas, and shallow waters of the oceans. How much is contributed to the atmosphere from these sources is not known for certain, but it is considerable. Estimates of naturally produced sulfates and other sulfur compounds are from 35 to 85 percent of the total—a rather wide range. And naturally occurring nitrogen compounds are generally believed to be 40 to 60 percent of the total. Some experts go further and say nature contributes more than 90 percent of global nitrogen. Considering the additional sulfur that emanates from volcanoes, fumaroles, hot springs, ocean spray, and the nitrogen fixed by lightning, the generally accepted contribution from natural sources may be underestimated.[7]

The contribution of lightning to the acidity of rain is significant. Two strokes of lightning over one square kilometer, or two-fifths of a square mile, produce enough nitric acid to make four-fifths of an inch of rain with a pH of 3.5. In fact, it has been estimated that lightning alone creates enough nitric acid to keep annual rainfall at a global average of pH 5.0.

The contribution of volcanoes to atmospheric sulfur dioxide seems never to have been taken seriously. It's been acknowledged, yes, but then dismissed as trivial. Perhaps this is related to the fact that volcanoes are studied by geologists and vulcanologists, rather than by atmospheric scientists. Or perhaps it's because volcanic mountains tend to be where meteorologists are not. Predicting exactly when an eruption will occur is notoriously difficult, and obtaining direct measurements or samples of ejecta during eruptions is dangerous and can be fatal.

During the daylong eruption of Mount St. Helens on May 18, 1980, more than four billion tons of material were ejected.[8] Although large quantities of gases, including sulfur dioxide, were released to the atmosphere, no direct measurements could be made during the major eruption itself. From March 29 to May 14, four days before the eruption, spectroscopic measurements revealed gaseous emissions of about 40 tons a day. On June 6 this increased abruptly to 1,000 tons a day. From the end of June through December of that year, the rates of sulfur dioxide ranged from 500 tons a day to 3,400 tons a day. Sulfur dioxide, hydrogen sulfide, carbon disulfide, and other sulfur compounds continue to be released from the crater floor and dome, and arise from fumaroles and the debris of pyroclastic flows.

El Chicon, an exceptionally acidic and sulfurous mountain in Mexico, erupted in early 1982, far more violently than Mount St. Helens. Its ejected materials reached the stratosphere, and will probably affect the atmosphere for many years. Again, no direct measurements were possible, but it is estimated that 20 billion tons of sulfur dioxide were released. Also, in the Northern Hemisphere, Mount St. Augustine in Alaska erupted twice in 1986, with sulfur fumes detectable in Anchorage, many miles away. Sulfur fumes have continued to seep from both El Chicon and St. Augustine.

In 1973, two scientists, Stoiber and Jepson,[9] reported data on sulfur dioxide emissions from Central American volcanoes, which they obtained by remote sensing and by calculation. They concluded that 10,000 metric tons of sulfur dioxide have been released to the atmosphere daily by these volcanoes. Extrapolating world-wide, they calculated that volcanoes are responsible for emitting about 100 million metric tons of sulfur compounds annually. Thus, nature is responsible for putting large quantities of sulfates and nitrates into the atmosphere.

Man-Made Sources

But so, of course, is man. Industrial activity, transportation, and burning fossil fuel for commercial and domestic purposes all contribute sulfate, nitrates, and other pollutants to the atmosphere. Since passage of the Clean Air Act of 1970, there has been an overall reduction of more than 40 percent in factory and utility sulfur dioxide production. But as sulfur dioxide emissions decrease, nitrogen emissions are increasing, primarily from oil burning and the oil used in transportation.

Industrial society also produces other air pollutants, including volatile organic compounds, ammonia, and hydrocarbons. Any of these may contribute to the formation of acid rain, either singly or in combination. Further, some man-made pollutants can undergo photo-oxidation in sunlight, leading, for example, to the conversion of sulfur dioxide to highly toxic sulfur trioxide. But even this compound, should it be deposited over the ocean, loses its toxicity due to the extraordinarily high buffering capacity of sea water.

Another photo-oxidant, ozone, is possibly the most damaging of all air pollutants derived from human activity. Ozone accumulates in quantities toxic to vegetation in all industrial regions of the world. It is a product of photochemical oxidation between oxides of nitrogen and volatile organic substances. The latter may be unburned hydrocarbons—for example, from automobile exhausts in cars not equipped with catalytic converters—or it may be various organic solvents. Ozone is known to cause severe injury and even death to certain forest trees. The best known cases are the decline of white pine in much of eastern North America and ponderosa and Jeffrey pine in the San Bernardino Mountains of California. Ozone acts synergistically with other pollutants and has been shown to cause damage to agricultural crops when exposure occurs along with sulfur and nitrogen oxides.

Thus, singling out sulfur dioxide produced by human activities as the major cause of acid rain is not only a gross oversimplification, but probably wrong.[10]

Effects on Forests

What about the dying forests? Here again the acid rain activists blame sulfur dioxide produced by industry. Like every other living thing, trees are not immortal. They, too, grow old and die. The decline of a forest may be part of the slow but natural process of plant succession, or it may be initiated by any of several stress-causing factors. Each forest and each tree species responds differently to environmental insults, whether natural or human. Professor Paul D. Mannion of the State University of New York, said this:[11]

> If one recognizes the complex array of factors that can contribute to the decline of trees, it is difficult to accept the hypothesis that air pollutants are the basis of our tree decline problems today . . . [although] to question the popular opinion on the cause of our decline problems is not to suggest that pollutants do not produce any effect.

Widespread mortality of forest trees has occurred at times and places where pollution stress was probably not a factor. Declines of western white pine in the 1930s and yellow birch in the 1940s and 1950s, for example, were induced by drought, while secondary invasion by insects or other disease organisms is most often the ultimate cause of fatality.

Currently, the most widely publicized forest decline problem in the U.S. is the red spruce forest in the northern Appalachian Mountains. Few people now cite the widespread mortality in red spruce between 1871 and 1890. The dieback occurred at roughly the same time in West Virginia, New York, Vermont, New Hampshire, Maine, and New Brunswick, and then was attributed to the invasion of a spruce beetle that followed upon some other stress inflicted upon the trees. What that stress was is not clear.

Today the dieback symptoms of the red spruce are most pronounced in areas 900 meters or more above sea level—an environment that is subject to natural stresses, such as wind, winter cold, and nutrient-poor soils, as well as possible high levels of pollutants, heavy metals, and acidity in the clouds that often envelop the forest. The relative importance of each of these stresses has not been rigorously investigated.

The affected trees grow in one of the windiest locations in North America. It is known that wind can dry out or even remove red spruce foliage, especially if rime ice has formed. It can also cause root damage by excessive tree movements. Tree ring analyses indicate a possible relation between recent cold winters and decline. The abnormal cold extending into spring may have caused the trees to be more susceptible to the adverse effects of pollutants.

Arthur H. Johnson and Samuel B. MacLaughlin, who have studied tree rings and the red spruce forest decline, wrote this in their *Acid Deposition: Long Term Trends*: "There is no indication now that acidic deposition is an important factor in red spruce decline. . . . The abrupt and synchronous changes in ring width and wood density patterns across such a wide area seem more likely to be related to climate than to air pollution."

In Germany, where acid precipitation, deposition of sulfur dioxide, and concentrations of nitrogen oxides were once thought to be killing the forests, emphasis has now shifted to the possible culpability of oxides of nitrogen, hydrocarbons, photo-oxidants (chiefly ozone), and such soil minerals as aluminum and magnesium. Sulfur dioxide emissions have been declining in Germany since the mid-1970s, due mainly to the substitution of nuclear energy for coal burning in the production of electricity. But this decline has not been accompanied by improvement in the health of forests, suggesting that other factors might be at work.[12] It is now believed that only in exceptional cases does sulfur dioxide cause direct damage to forests in Germany. But German motor vehicle pollution from more than 27 million cars and trucks is among the highest in the world and is considered to be a contributing factor to the formation of ozone. Indeed, ozone levels in Germany's damaged forests are often remarkably high. Long-term measurements indicate that the mean value of ozone concentration has increased by one-third over the last 20 years. And the investigators at the Norwegian Forest Institute have reached similar conclusions about the importance of ozone in forest declines.

The catalytic converter was adopted for automobiles in America primarily to control the release of unburned hydrocarbons and reduce the photochemical production of ozone. In this it has functioned well, although it has also led to formation of formaldehyde and larger amounts of acid, especially sulfuric acid. But there is another source of atmospheric hydrocarbons that has not been controlled—cows! American cows burp about 50 million tons of hydrocarbons into the atmosphere annually! There is no known control technology for these emissions. Whether they contribute to ozone formation is also not known, but their presence helps to emphasize the complexity of atmospheric chemistry.

Effects on Lakes and Fish[13]

There are three kinds of naturally occurring acidic lakes. First are those associated with inorganic acids in geothermal areas, like Yellowstone Park, and sulfur springs, with a pH of 2.0 to 3.0. Then there are those found in peat lands, cypress swamps, and rain forests, where the acidity is derived from organic acids leached from humus and decaying vegetation, with pH 3.5 to 5. Finally, there are those in areas of weather-resistant granitic or silicious bedrock, which are the only ones involved in the acid rain question.

In these lakes and streams, the absence of carbonate rocks means little natural buffering capacity. This type of naturally acidic lake is common in large areas of eastern Canada and the northeastern United States, where glaciers exposed granitic bedrock during the last period of glaciation. The lakes are called "sensitive" because they may readily become further acidified with adverse effects on aquatic organisms, of which fish are the most important to man. Indeed, the most widely proclaimed complaint about acid deposition is the reduction or elimination of fish populations.

But again, this is not a recent phenomenon. Dead lakes are not new. A study by the New York State Department of Environmental Conservation reveals that the stocking of fish in 12 lakes was attempted and failed as early as the 1920s. Of course, many people did catch fish in the 1920s and 1930s in lakes where fish are not available today. But the fact is that during those years many of the Adirondack lakes were being stocked annually by the Fish and Game Commission. Fish did not propagate, and the stocking program was discontinued about 1940.

In the United States, 219 lakes have been identified as too acidic to support fish. Two hundred and six of these lakes are in the Adirondacks, but they account for only four percent of the lake surface of New York State. This, then, is hardly a national problem; it is local. The same applies to southeastern Canada, which has the highest percentage of acid lakes.

Scientists are uncertain whether these acid lakes have always had a low pH or whether human activities have reduced the neutralizing capability of the waters or the lake basin. A range of human activities could be to blame—use of chemical pesticides to control spruce budworm or black fly infestations, changes in fish hatchery production and increased demand for fish, burning of watersheds, and logging. On the other hand, declining fish populations were noted in some New York lakes as early as 1918, and bottom sediments deposited 800 years ago in Scandinavian lakes are more acid than today's sediments.

To conclude that a decline in fish population is caused by atmospheric acid deposition, it must be established that the lake formerly supported a viable fish population, that one or more species of fish formerly present have been reduced or lost, that the lake is more acidic now than it was when the fish were present, that an increase in acid level was not caused by local factors, and that other factors, such as toxic chemicals, are not present or are not important. Such data are rare. Studies on three lakes in the Adirondacks—Panther, Sagamore, and Woods Lake, which are remote but close enough together to be affected by the same rainfall—disclosed radically different degrees of acidity, large differences that can be accounted for by the varying geological makeup of the three lake beds and local surrounding soils and vegetation.

Outside the Adirondack Mountains and New York State, many emotional claims have been made about fish kills in Canada, Norway, and Sweden. Most of the losses are reported in the spring. In Scandinavia, fish kills have been reported annually in the springtime for more than 100 years. This recurring natural phenomenon is probably due to oxygen depletion or to snow melt and rain runoff carrying sudden high concentrations of many materials into lakes and streams, and, in fact, the acidity of most waters is greatest in the spring. Modern findings call into question the claim that distant sources of sulfur dioxide are responsible for the growing acidity of waters hundreds of miles away.

Using trace elements, Dr. Kenneth Rahn of the University of Rhode Island has found that local pollution sources, mostly residual fuel oil burned for domestic, commercial, and industrial purposes in New England, are the main cause of added acidity in rain and snow. A meteorological team from the University of Stockholm cautioned Swedes not to blame acid rain on emissions from England. They found that local sources accounted for local acid rain. Great Britain, incidentally, has reduced sulfur dioxide emissions by more than 30 percent since 1970, with no effect whatever on the acidity of lakes or rain in Scandinavia. In New York City, Environmental Protection Agency scientists traced elevated sulfur dioxide and sulfuric acid in the wintertime to the burning of oil in the 35,000 oil burners of the city's apartment houses. European scientists at the Organization for Economic and Cooperative Development in Paris have concluded, in the most revealing result of an extensive project, that every source region affects itself more than any other region.

Effects on Man-Made Structures

The impact of airborne pollutants and acid rain on deterioration of buildings, monuments, and man-made materials is also predominantly a local phenomenon. It is at least as complex as the effects on the natural environment. And, like forests and lakes, every site is specific and every material different. Few generalizations are possible. Fewer still stand up under careful scrutiny. Of course metals corrode, marble and limestone weather, masonry and concrete deteriorate, paint erodes, and so on. But the conditions and substances that lead to loss of integrity vary widely. Perhaps the only statements that can be made are that moisture is essential, that deterioration results more from acid deposition than from acid rain, and that local pollutants are more important than pollutants possibly transported from far away.

Yet the belief persists that acid rain from "someplace else" is destroying cultural monuments and buildings. Perhaps the most egregious example is the damage to the granite Egyptian obelisk, "Cleopatra's Needle," which has been in New York's Central Park since 1881. It's been said that "the city's atmosphere has done more damage than three and a half millenia in the desert, and in another dozen years the hieroglyphs will disappear." A careful study of the monument's complex history, however, makes it clear that the damage can be attributed to advanced salt decay from the "salting" of icy streets during winter, the high humidity of the New York climate in the summer, and unfortunate attempts at preservation. There is no question but that acid deposition causes incremental damage to materials, but far more research is needed before reliable surface protection systems can be developed.

Congress should be very cautious about committing public funds to "solutions" to an ill-defined problem. At best, proposed federal programs constitute, in the words of Dr. S. Fred Singer of the National Advisory Committee on Oceans and Atmosphere, "a multibillion dollar solution to a multimillion dollar problem."[14]

One federal program that fits this description is a plan to pool $2.5 billion of federal funds with $2.5 billion from American industry for a project that would demonstrate how to burn high sulfur coal and release less sulfur dioxide to the atmosphere. Burning low sulfur coal was not proposed because that would "impose significant socio-economic costs on high sulfur coal miners, their families, and their communities."

Industrial activities generally and coal burning in particular put pollutants into the atmosphere, and what goes up must come down . . . somewhere. It's reasonable, therefore, to require, as the Clean Air Act does, that emissions of sulfur dioxide and other pollutants be reduced. It's also reasonable to spend federal funds to collect accurate data and to continue efforts to understand the problem of acid deposition in all its complexity. What is *not* reasonable is the requirement by a Congress impatient for immediate results that all coal-burning utilities must use expensive flue gas scrubbers, regardless of whether the coal complies with federal standards.

With even less reason, the 1977 amendments to the Clean Air Act require that the sulfur content of all coal be reduced by the same percentage. It seems not to matter, under this law, that low sulfur Western coal still goes into the scrubbers cleaner than high sulfur Eastern coal comes out of them. What apparently does matter is that the top eight polluting states have large high sulfur coal reserves and high economic dependence on mining it. They are represented in the House of Representatives by 105 votes. In contrast, Western low sulfur coal is dominated by two states, Montana, with two votes, and Wyoming, with one.

Does our knowledge about acid rain, its origin, extent, and effect on the environment, warrant spending 2.5 billion or more taxpayer dollars on a program to reduce atmospheric SO_2? There are plenty of good reasons to cut down on the amount of sulfur and other pollutants that pour into the atmosphere, but to use acid rain as an excuse and to intimate that if SO_2 is eliminated then acid rain will disappear is not only simplistic and unscientific, it is grossly misleading, as well.

Yet that is what the federal government has done. Urged on by his image-conscious staff and reports on acid rain problems in southeastern Canada, and apparently motivated more by politics than by scientific evidence, the President would have us believe that if enough money were spent to devise ways to reduce SO_2 in the effluent from the stacks of Midwestern coal-burning utilities, the acid rain problems would go away. They won't. But that is what the most recent amendments to the Clean Air Act would require.

As already discussed, atmospheric SO_2—which is widely assumed, but certainly not proved, to be the primary cause of acid rain—has been reduced by more than 15 percent since 1973. Yet the acidity of rainwater remains the same. Similar results with even greater SO_2 reductions (30 percent since 1970) are reported from Great Britain and Scandinavia. Most knowledgeable scientists agree that about half of all atmospheric sulfur worldwide comes from natural causes, including volcanic eruptions. We also know that rainwater is naturally acidic; that its acidity can be increased by pollutants; that the amount of acid deposition—which is much more important than the pH of rainwater—and the natural pH of soils differs widely across the United

States; and that naturally occurring limestone, the liming of agricultural soil, and the use of ammonia-based fertilizers buffer acid deposition.

That the consequences of acid deposition can be adverse is well established, but they are local and regional, not universal. Extensive research by the Organization for Economic Cooperation and Development has shown that "every source region affects itself more than any other region." This is true also for New England and southeastern Canada.

If those who insist that their acid rain problems come from coal-burning utilities in the Ohio Valley were serious about solving the problem, they would insist on proof. Proof could easily be obtained by adding small amounts of a tracer (radioactive isotope Sulfur-35) to the smoke of utility burners and seeing whether the sulfur-bearing plume actually reaches New England in significant amounts.

If those who call for penalizing coal-burning utilities were really sincere, they would be campaigning vigorously for conversion to nuclear power. Nuclear power plants emit no sulfur, no nitrogen, no CO_2, no organic compounds, and only a tiny amount of radioactivity, less than 0.1 percent of the natural level. Coal burners emit all of these, including unknown amounts of unregulated, uncontrolled radioactivity.

What to do?[15] Any federal funds that will be spent on acid rain should be spent on research—not on boondoggles to satisfy the mindless cries to "do something" from those who would substitute passion for science.[16]

Chapter 6

"ACID RAIN" FOR INSECTS: PESTICIDES

NO CONSIDERATION OF PESTICIDES and their role in public health and agriculture would be complete without recounting the story of DDT. The events surrounding its use, overuse, and its being banned in the U.S. are dramatic. DDT was the first, best, and most remarkable of modern pesticides. Its history is a tale of triumph that ended in tragedy.

DDT, the convenient name for 1,1,1-trichloro-2,2-bis (p-chlorophenyl) ethane, was first synthesized in 1877 and patented as an insecticide in 1939 by a Swiss chemist, Dr. Paul Muller. Its remarkable effectiveness against insects, specifically clothes moths and ectoparasites of both animals and plants, made it a welcome substitute for the toxic insecticides then in common use—arsenic, mercury, fluorine, and lead. In 1942, it was shown to kill body lice without adverse effect on humans, and it was used by all Allied troops during World War II.[1] The result was that no Allied soldier was stricken with typhus fever (carried by lice) for the first time in the history of warfare. In World War I, by contrast, more soldiers died from typhus than from bullets.

Mosquito-borne malaria has always been man's worst disease, judged by the number of its victims. Until DDT came along, about

200 million people were stricken annually with malaria, and about two million of them died each year.[2] Beginning in 1946, a large-scale spraying program directed against the malaria-carrying mosquito brought an immediate and dramatic decrease in these numbers. It is important to emphasize that this spraying was not indiscriminate, nor was it conducted in the natural environment. It was performed inside homes, on the interior walls. The unique behavior of the malarial mosquito—feeding at night on sleeping victims and then flying to the nearest vertical structure to rest and digest its meal—made this the ideal way to catch the largest number of adult insects.

Public health statistics from Sri Lanka testify to the effectiveness of the spraying program. In 1948, before use of DDT, there were 2.8 million cases of malaria. By 1963, there were only 17. Low levels of infection continued until the late 1960s, when the attacks on DDT in the U.S. convinced officials to suspend spraying. In 1968, there were one million cases of malaria. In 1969, the number reached 2.5 million, back to the pre-DDT levels.[3] Moreover, by 1972, the largely unsubstantiated charges against DDT in the United States had a worldwide effect. In 1970, of two billion people living in malarial regions, 79 percent were protected and the expectation was that malaria would be eradicated. Six years after the United States banned DDT, there were 800 million cases of malaria and 8.2 million deaths per year. Even worse, because eradication programs were halted at a critical time, resistant malaria is now widespread and travelers could take it home. Much of the southern United States is favorable to the malarial mosquito. Malaria, yellow fever, and other diseases for which mosquitoes are the vector, used to be endemic in the South; mosquitoes have recently undergone an explosive population growth since their breeding grounds are now "protected" under federal law.

In 1948, Dr. Muller was awarded the Nobel Prize in medicine because of the medical importance of DDT. Dr. Samuel Simmons, chief of the technology branch of the Communicable Disease Center of the U.S. Public Health Service, said in 1959:[4]

The total value of DDT to mankind is inestimable. Most of the peoples of the globe have received benefit from it either directly by protection from infectious diseases and pestiferous insects or indirectly by better nutrition, cleaner food, and increased disease resistance. The discovery of DDT will always remain an historic event in the fields of public health and agriculture.

After initial success in controlling typhus and malaria, DDT was also used against yellow fever, sleeping sickness, plague, and encephalitis, all transmitted by insects and all epidemic at various times in the past in the United States.

"With the introduction of DDT to control the vectors of disease," wrote Claus and Bolander in 1977,[5] "it seemed, for the first time in history, that man could look forward to a life of dignity, freed from the scourges of maiming disease and famine. It is no wonder, then, that its applications were greeted with general high enthusiasm."

Was the prospect of more people living better also anathema to the population-control and zero-growth organizations? There is some reason to believe so.[6]

Plant pests also succumbed to DDT. It proved effective against spruce budworm, gypsy moth, tussock moth, pine weevil, and cotton boll weevil. So effective was DDT against such a variety of insects that it was inevitably overused. The attitude, "if a little bit is good, then more must be better," is a common human failing. Before any steps were taken to curtail and control DDT, it became ubiquitous in soil, water, and in the bodies of many living organisms. Even though no harm has ever been demonstrated to have been caused by DDT, its widespread presence in the environment was enough to give rise to alarm.

Contrary to common belief, DDT is not a persistent pesticide in the natural environment. Only in the unusual circumstances where soil is dark, dry, and devoid of microorganisms will DDT persist. Under normal environmental conditions, DDT loses its toxicity to insects in a few days, usually no more than two weeks. But its overuse did result in DDT being detected, albeit in small amounts, in soil, in water both salt and fresh, in the bodies of fish, birds, and domestic animals, and in man. This energized the opposition to its use that had first been sparked by the lyrical hysteria of Rachel Carson's book, *Silent Spring*.[7]

The growing chorus from self-proclaimed environmentalists demanding that DDT be totally banned led to a public hearing in 1971. It should be noted that the Environmental Protection Agency, the agency responsible for regulating pesticides and for making the final decision about their use, actually took part in the hearing, testifying against DDT, along with the Environmental Defense Fund and other activist groups. The attack on DDT rested on three main allegations: that DDT caused the death of many birds and could lead to the extinction of some bird populations; that DDT was so stable that it could never be eliminated from the environment, and that DDT might cause cancer in humans. None of these charges has ever been substantiated.

It was alleged that DDT was toxic to birds that might ingest it from eating insects, earthworms, or seeds in sprayed areas. It was also charged that sub-lethal amounts of DDT in the bodies of birds caused them to lay eggs with thin shells that provided insufficient protection, resulting in the death of many chicks. These charges have been repeated so often that they are widely believed, even though they are, at best, "factoids," untrue in most instances.

Actual counts of bird populations, conducted annually by the Audubon Society at Christmastime, have shown that many bird populations were in fact increasing throughout the years of heaviest DDT spraying.[8] For example, between 1941 and 1971, there was a 12 percent increase in robins, 21 times more cowbirds, 8 times more blackbirds, and 131 times more grackles. Gulls also increased, especially along the East Coast. Aside from robins—possibly America's most abundant bird, which some hysterical environmentalists said was "doomed" by DDT—it is the birds of prey that caught most of the anti-DDT attention, especially the osprey and the peregrine falcon. At the Hawk Mountain Sanctuary in Pennsylvania, annual surveys show 191 ospreys in 1946, compared to 600 in 1970. Each year showed some population increase. For the peregrine falcon, the numbers fluctuated from a low of 14 in 1965 to a high of 32 in 1969. Dr. Joseph Hickey, an authority on peregrines, testified at the DDT hearings that the falcon population had been declining since 1890. Its fate is more closely related to the availability of prey and nesting sites than to pesticides. For all hawks, the annual counts showed an increase from 9,291 in

1957 to 20,196 in 1967. Since it was protected by the endangered species designation, populations of the American Bald Eagle have increased significantly. Although environmentalists claim that this resurgence is due to banning DDT, there is no supportive evidence.

In the case of thin egg shells, it is a phenomenon that predates use of DDT. It has been known for decades. There are many causes: diets low in calcium or Vitamin D, fright, high nocturnal temperatures, various toxic substances, and diseases such as Newcastle's disease. Experiments designed to show a toxic effect from eating DDT failed, even though the experimenters fed their birds (pheasant and quail) from 6,000 to 20,000 times more DDT than the 0.3 parts per million residue of DDT found in food. Quail fed 200 parts per million in all their food throughout the reproductive period nevertheless hatched 80 percent of their chicks, compared with an 84 percent hatch in the control groups. No shell-thinning was reported. With pheasants handled in the same way, the DDT-treated birds hatched 80.6 percent of their eggs, compared with only 57.4 percent in the control groups.

DDT rapidly breaks down harmlessly in the natural environment. But in 1968, when DDT was still in wide use, a residue detected in food was measurable. An average daily human intake could reach 0.065 milligrams. To study the effect on humans, volunteer groups were fed up to 35 milligrams of DDT per day for periods of 21 and 27 months, with no ill effects then or in the nearly 30 years since. Most of the DDT is excreted, with some small residue, up to 12 parts per million, stored in human fat. No harm whatsoever has been detected from these trivial amounts. In sea water, which ultimately receives all the runoff from the land, more than 93 percent of all DDT is broken down in 38 days, but one part per *trillion* can be detected in inshore waters. Compare this to the irresponsible and unscientific claim by butterfly specialist and environmental guru Paul Ehrlich who charged that DDT in sea water would kill all algae (phytoplankton) and thus deprive the earth of 40 percent of its oxygen.

Finally, as for DDT being a cancer-causing agent, if one concludes that all growths, even benign tumors and lumps, are cancer, then the answer must be yes, but. . . . The "but" is important. If one accepts as "cancer" only malignant growths that can metastisize, then the answer is an unequivocal no. DDT is not a carcinogen. Laboratory studies have reported liver deformations in mice, but not in any other experimental animal (including rats). This is the basis for the charge that DDT is "cancer-causing." The doses, given by injection, required to cause the deformation of a mouse's liver were about 100,000 times higher than any possible ingestion from DDT residues in food.

The National Cancer Institute reviewed the mouse experiment results and, in 1978, declared DDT was not a carcinogen. It is also interesting to note that deaths from liver cancer in the United States actually *decreased* by 30 percent during the years of heaviest DDT use (1944 to 1972). Moreover, millions of people were exposed to DDT during the malarial spraying programs, and those who did the spraying, 130,000 men, were exposed to high concentrations with no ill effects.

These data and much more were presented at the 1971 hearing and the recommendation, after considering 300 technical documents and the testimony of 150 scientists, was that a total ban on DDT was not desirable, based on the scientific evidence. The hearing examiner declared in his final decision: "There is a present need for the continued use of DDT for the essential uses defined in this case."[9]

That was in April 1972. Nevertheless, two months later, on June 14, 1972, William Ruckelshaus, EPA administrator, banned all uses of DDT unless an essential public purpose could be proved. Why did he do it? Two years earlier, Ruckelshaus had stated his support of DDT, citing its "amazing and exemplary record of safe use." Was he trying to curry favor with the environmental activist organizations? (When he left the EPA, he signed membership solicitation letters for the Environmental Defense Fund, the organization that led the fight against DDT.) Or was he trying to demonstrate muscle and establish the power of the EPA?

Years later, Ruckelshaus admitted that "decisions by the government involving the use of toxic substances are political . . . [and] the ultimate judgment remains political. . . . [In] the case of pesticides, the power to make this judgment has been delegated to the Administrator of EPA."[10]

The banning of DDT could not be justified on scientific grounds—

regulation yes, control yes, but a total ban no. Had Ruckelshaus taken that position, instead of prohibition, back in 1972, we would still have the benefits of this important chemical today. The most important fallout from the Ruckelshaus decision on DDT was that it gave credibility to *pseudoscience*, it created an atmosphere in which scientific evidence can be pushed aside by emotion, hysteria, and political pressure. It has done inestimable damage. The technique of making unsubstantiated charges, endlessly repeated, has since been used successfully against asbestos, PCBs, dioxin, and, of course, Alar.

DDT and other insecticides, herbicides, fungicides, and rodenticides have had a tremendous effect on agriculture. So, indeed, have other chemicals, fertilizers, improved varieties of crops, and better understanding of soil treatment and crop management. All of these, in an informed, integrated program of pest management, have led to an abundance in food production undreamed of a few decades ago. Never again need there be a disaster like the famine in the 1840s in Ireland that was caused by a fungus, Fusarium, the late potato blight. That catastrophe led to the death of one third of Ireland's population from starvation, another third emigrated, and the bitterness that exists between the Irish and the English was intensified yet further. How much of the tragedy of the Emerald Isle might have been averted if a good fungicide like captan had been available?

The potato makes a good object lesson for those who think "nature knows best" and who believe manure and crop rotation are all that's needed.[11] In the 1920s, given good soil and animal fertilizer, an exceptional yield was 75 100-pound sacks of potatoes per acre. By 1940, the best methods were producing 82 sacks per acre. Then came the introduction of modern agriculture, with its chemicals and pesticides. The results look like this:

Year	100-Pound Sacks Per Acre
1950	165
1960	208
1970	247
1980s	275

The dramatic increase didn't happen without help—from technology. With the very modern problem of agricultural surpluses in this country, we forget that in the 6,000 years of known human history, such food surpluses are new and unique.

In the 1930s, soil erosion became a serious problem in the United States, dramatized by the "dust bowl" experience in the farm areas of the Midwest. Contour plowing, windbreaks, and better soil management helped, but the most important innovation involved the introduction of herbicides for weed control, thereby making extensive tillage and disturbance of the soil unnecessary.

Pesticides have reduced America's food costs 33 percent by controlling weeds, insects, mold, and rot in vegetables and fruits. They have helped to keep our food and our homes clean by controlling rats, mice, and cockroaches. Through the use of wood preservatives in pressure-treated lumber for fences, porches, decks, and homes, we have saved a forest of trees two times the size of New England.

Modern agriculture has made it possible to grow more food, poultry, dairy products, and fiber on less land. This means that more land can be returned to woodlot, forest, and recreational uses. Of the 3.6 million square miles that constitute the United States, 32 percent—or 1.13 million square miles—are forests or woodlots.[12] Because of this, the average annual wood growth is now three and a half times more than it was in 1920. Tree-growing areas increased 18 percent from 1952 to 1977. Forests in America continue to increase in size, even while supplying a substantial portion of the world's timber needs. Better forest management, improved seedlings, and informed use of fertilizers and pesticides have made this possible. The main danger to our forests today comes from federal lands (national parks, national forests, and wilderness areas), where no management is allowed, because "nature knows best." They now serve as foci for the production and dissemination of forest pests.

The fact is, we are about 10,000 years past the point where we can consider any part of nature untouched by humans or their activities. We cannot return to that faraway time. Besides, most farms maintain uncropped areas that are important to perpetuate wildlife, and there are more than two million farm ponds in the United States where wild species thrive.

By nature, plants require many different elements to survive and grow. But nature did not distribute these elements evenly. It is up to man to supply them. For *good* plant growth, calcium, phosphorus, potassium, magnesium, and nitrogen all must be supplied. This is the function of fertilizer. The ammonia arising from cattle urine is the same as that supplied from a chemical solution. It is a myth that "man-made" or synthetic compounds are dangerous and toxic, whereas the same compounds found in nature—for example, "natural chemicals"—are safe. There is no chemical difference between them.

But ignorant opponents of all man's efforts to improve human life on this earth have continued to insist that extremely low levels of industrial chemicals can be toxic or carcinogenic and that everything "synthetic" is somehow uniquely dangerous and will cause cancer. This is not true. It is the *dose*—the size or amount of exposure—that is important. The amount of natural pesticides we eat every day is at least 10,000 times the level of pesticide residue from agricultural use of synthetics.[13]

Arsenic, cadmium, and chromium are all officially identified as carcinogens, yet they are all naturally present in every cell in our bodies. How much arsenic do we normally have? One hundred thousand molecules per cell. How much cadmium? Two million molecules per cell. How much chromium? Seven hundred thousand per cell. To believe, as the "one molecule can cause cancer" adherents do, that one extra molecule out of several hundred thousand will disrupt the DNA molecule and cause cancer stretches credulity beyond imagination. The theory, to put it bluntly, is nonsensical scare-mongering.[14]

People, however, are attracted to horror stories, and since the news media are primarily in the entertainment business, scientific accuracy has a very low priority. At a recent symposium sponsored by the Smithsonian Institution, Ben Bradlee, editor of *The Washington Post*, said: "To hell with the news! I'm no longer interested in news. I'm interested in causes. We don't print the truth. We don't pretend to print the truth. We print what people tell us. It's up to the public to decide what's true."[15]

Careful studies have established that 99.99 percent of the carcinogenic materials ingested daily are either natural or produced by drinking alcohol, cooking, or smoking. The simple way to avoid any problem is to eat a balanced diet with a reasonable variety of different foods. To avoid consuming carcinogens or other toxic substances, one would have to refrain from eating carrots, radishes, onions, olives, melons, ham, shrimp, potatoes, parsley, butter rolls, broccoli, watercress, avocado, lemons, cheese, bananas, apples, oranges, tea, milk, wine, water, and much else besides.

Nitrite, nitrate, and nitrosamines can be avoided only by eliminating most vegetables, especially beets, celery, lettuce, radishes, rhubarb, mustard kale, turnips, cabbage, and. . . .

Well, it gets silly. Yet, if any of these foods were subject to tests similar to those used to screen synthetic chemicals, they would all be banned.

Chapter 7

THE ALAR, ASBESTOS, PCB, AND DIOXIN SCARES

I N THE FACE of all the evidence that proper use of synthetic pesticides and fertilizers has produced enormous benefits to human health and nutrition, it is difficult to understand the campaign to eliminate them. There is already a well planned effort under way to arouse public fear and force rejection of food grown with pesticides or any manufactured chemical. The opening skirmish has already been won; it was the carefully orchestrated attack on apples treated with Alar.[1] The Alar victory has encouraged the environmental extremists. The Natural Resources Defense Council (NRDC) is spearheading a movement in California to ban 24 agricultural chemicals that are now in use, and a new organization called the National Toxics Campaign is pressuring supermarkets to join an effort to ban *all* chemical pesticides and fertilizers.[2]

Was the attack on Alar justified? Extensive studies carried out with scrupulous attention to scientific protocol have failed to find any credible evidence that Alar causes cancer. Extrapolating to humans from the NRDC mouse tests, a person would have to eat 28,000 pounds of apples every day for 70 years to produce tumors similar to those suffered by mice exposed to megadoses of Alar. What the NRDC did not include in its well publicized attack on Alar was that mice fed half the maximum amount—which would equal a man's eating 14,000 pounds of apples a day for 70 years—produced no tumors at all.[3]

The anti-Alar attack did produce fright that in some cases bordered on panic, and grocers removed apples from their shelves for fear of reprisals. The apple-growing industry lost more than $200 million and the wholesale price of a box dropped below the production cost; some growers may not recover. The EPA succumbed to pressure and decertified Alar because of that pressure, *not* because of any scientific data. As a result, Uniroyal Chemical Company, the only producer of Alar, removed it from the market.

The ensuing year's crop of apples, devoid of Alar, showed less firmness and color; the McIntosh crop was down and some Stayman and Winesap varieties bore signs of splitting skins. Apples are not an easy crop to market. Many varieties bruise too easily or deteriorate too rapidly to stand even a few weeks of storage. Apples need all the help they can get.[4]

Alar is not a pesticide. It is a growth regulator that helps to keep apples on the tree longer, thus promoting development of a deeper red color and more crispness. It also made harvesting more uniform and economic. Dr. John A. Moore, the acting EPA administrator at the time, has since said that the NRDC report was "gravely misleading," because it was "rejected in scientific peer review" and contained food consumption data of "unproved validity."[5]

"In the Alar case," he added, "the public was very prone to give credence to the selective and inappropriate use of data regarding consumer risks and to believe 'the worst,' despite a counter-statement by the EPA."[6]

Unjustified as it was, the attack on Alar was sophisticated, carried out with maximum publicity, and successful.

To repeat a most important point, of all the pesticide residues we eat, 99.99 percent of them are natural. Domestication of vegetables and fruits has led, through selection, to the emergence of varieties that contain fewer natural pesticides and toxic substances than their "wild-type" original species. This has been going on for 10,000 years—since the beginning of agriculture, when human beings started to transform wild plants into more productive crops with fewer toxic side effects. One of the important effects of domestication has been to reduce the level of toxic constituents of potatoes, lettuce, lima beans, cabbage, and other foods to tolerable levels. In an excess of enthusiasm for "natural" pesticides, researchers have developed a strain of potato that is resistant to insect pests. It is also so toxic to humans (because of an increase in the naturally occurring alkaloid chemicals chaconine and solanin) that it has been withdrawn. The same thing is true for an insect-resistant strain of celery; it causes dermatitis.[7]

There is also the recurring fad for "natural" foods and "organically grown" foods. Many environmental organizations have espoused "organic" (by which they mean "primitive") agriculture—using only animal excreta for fertilizer, natural predators for pesticides, practicing crop rotation, and mulching. This is now called "alternative agriculture"; it is nothing more than the use of pre-technology growing techniques, which are promoted as being somehow more "pure." Apparently even the U.S. Department of Agriculture has been taken in.[8] Probably it is the department's most recent attempt to contain farm surpluses, because without doubt much less food can be grown "organically" than through the use of modern technology.

The "natural food" fad is not new. Suggesting, as it does, a fundamental harmony, a condition of purity and simplicity, the idea has always had great appeal. The history of the idea of naturalness derives from Jean-Jacques Rousseau, who said in 1762,[9] "The more we depart from the state of nature, the more we lose our natural tastes," and, perhaps anticipating modern environmental nature worshippers, "All is good coming from the hand of the Author of all things; all degenerates in the hands of man."

Actually, the present interest in "organic food" and related nutritional fads, such as vegetarianism, is the second go-around in America. We were in fact genuine pioneers in this field, with the first flowering occurring 150 years ago. It was then that Sylvester Graham promoted his whole grain flours (Graham crackers) and John Harvey Kellogg introduced breakfast cereals.[10] Graham, a Presbyterian preacher, promoted his nutrition ideas in the 1830s, just as French aristocrat Alexis de Tocqueville was touring America. De Tocqueville wrote: "It is strange to see with what feverish ardor the Americans pursue their own welfare, and to watch the vague dread that torments them lest they should not have chosen the shortest path which may lead to it."[11]

He could have been writing about environmentalist dietary fads, which seem to offer a short cut to health and long life. America does seem peculiarly hospitable to dietary fads from low cholesterol to saturated fat, no salt, and plenty of bran and oatmeal flakes.

Vegetarian diets have always had a certain faddish popularity and are to be found among some religious cults (Zen), as well as those seeking long life through nutrition. Benjamin Franklin was one of the latter until he found himself becalmed on a ship where the crew caught cod and fried them. Franklin wrote in his autobiography (1691) with his usual pragmatic candor:[12]

> It smelt admirably well. I balanced some time between Principle and Inclination: till I recollected that when the fish were opened, I saw smaller Fish taken out of their Stomachs. Then, thought I, if you eat one another, I don't see why we mayn't eat you. So I dined upon Cod very heartily and continued to eat with other People, returning only now and then occasionally to a vegetable Diet. So convenient a thing it is to be a *reasonable Creature*, since it enables one to find or make a Reason for every thing one has a mind to do.

Today's vegetarians and animal rights advocates do not always reveal so reasonable a nature. The Animal Liberation Front, the militant arm of the animal rights movement, has joined with the ecology terrorist group called Earth First! to commit sabotage against poultry farms, cattle and sheep ranches, and animal feed lots in the West. They are also responsible for an increasing number of arson fires in livestock auction barns and headquarters. The Animal Liberation Front took credit for a fire in 1987 that destroyed the $2.5 million research center at the University of California at Davis. The Front's goal is the elimination of the livestock industry, and it is quite candid in saying so.[13]

Says Richard Simmonds, director of animal research for the University of Nevada, "It's an extremely serious problem. These people want to wipe out the meat industry, want to end the manufacture of leather and wool products."

A member of Earth First! who would not identify himself told *The Los Angeles Times*:

> I shot holes in the oil reservoirs on the gear boxes of windmills. When the wind blows after a day or two, it burns up the gears and destroys the gear box. I've thrown rocks and steel into wells to plug them. There are hundreds of galvanized steel water tanks all over the place. I've shot holes in them and pulled out float valves. I want to run ranchers out of business. [14]

Richard Whitaker of the FBI office in Las Vegas, Nevada, attributes increasing terrorist attacks to the teaming up of militant vegetarians with radical environmentalists. [15] This might be dismissed as paranoia were it not for the blatant promotion of the Earth First! book entitled *Ecodefense: A Field Guide to Monkeywrenching*, [16] now in its second edition and third printing. Its aim is coercive and its recommended actions are subversive.

What motivation drives these activists who try to force others to their lifestyle and ways of thinking? Are they deliberately trying to cripple American agriculture and the chemical industry? Do they hope to eventually decrease human population growth through famine? Or are they simply naive or misinformed or ignorant of what it takes to grow abundant food and protect public health? These questions should be asked of the radical environmentalists, because there are now approximately 60 to 100 million people who are dying each year as the direct or indirect result of anti-pesticide campaigns that have caused restrictions or bans on the products that could have prevented such deaths.

Nature is not kind to humans who abandon science and technology. There is nothing "natural" about large-scale farming or raising herds of domestic animals. There is nothing "natural" about human populations living close together, with their inevitable pests and vermin. Without deliberate human intervention, nature would soon eradicate the world's food producing capacity and unleash plagues of long forgotten virulence. Huge numbers of humans would suffer and die. Is that what the ban-all-pesticides environmentalists want?

Asbestos[17]

It has been known for many years that breathing asbestos fibers could lead to a serious lung disease, asbestosis, or even to lung cancer. In 1978, a mimeographed report, called a "Draft-Summary," was released jointly by the National Cancer Institute and the National Institute of Environment Health Sciences. It was titled "Estimates of the Fraction of Cancer Incidence in the United States Attributable to Occupational Factors."[18] Curiously, it listed no authors. Nine examples of occupational carcinogens were cited, including asbestos, for which it projected a shocking two million premature cancer deaths over the coming three decades. Previous projections had predicted 2,000 cancer deaths.

Joseph Califano, then secretary of the Department of Health, Education, and Welfare, used the "Draft-Summary" in a speech to organized labor at the AFL-CIO national conference. Quoting from the report, he told American labor that "5 million American men and women breathe significant amounts of asbestos fibers every day," and, in a remarkable extrapolation from the data, "17 percent of all cancer deaths in the U.S. every year will be associated with previous exposure to asbestos." No wonder that a fire storm of reaction against asbestos and its producers and manufacturers resulted.

The Manville Corporation, the country's largest producer of asbestos, was forced into bankruptcy.[19] It has set up a Personal Injury Settlement Trust, from which it has already paid for 5,000 settlements and faces an estimated 50,000 more. The Trust is expected to pay out at least $2.5 billion over the next 20 to 25 years, and it has pledged 20 percent of its profits and 80 percent of its stock for this purpose.

More recently, William Reilly, administrator of the EPA, has banned virtually all uses of asbestos by 1997 and many of them by 1993. This action was taken even though there are important products in which asbestos is essential; for example, automobile brake linings and protective gear for firefighters, for which there is no satisfactory substitute material available. The EPA has also ordered that asbestos be removed from the nation's public buildings, including about 45,000 schools. [20]

Are these drastic actions really necessary to protect the public health? To answer that question, a much closer look at the problem is necessary, beginning with the "Draft-Summary" of 1978.

When this remarkable, anonymous document was made public, the question of authorship was immediately raised, and both the methodology and conclusions were roundly criticized by scientists in the U.S. and abroad. After some delay, a list of names from the responsible agencies was appended to the "draft" as contributors, but no responsible author has ever been identified. Nor has the "Draft-Summary" ever been published or subjected to peer review; it went directly from a mimeograph to the HEW secretary to the labor conference and public knowledge. Its conclusions differ widely from all previous studies, as was pointed out by cancer specialists and epidemiologists. Criticism of the report, after an initial outcry, was muted in the U.S., but John Cairns, head of the Mill Hill Laboratory in London summed up the general reaction of scientists abroad when he said, "There are several parts of it which seem to be manifestly silly. Anyone who can perform calculations can see how stupid it is."[21]

In 1981, a most detailed attack on the "Draft-Summary" (now called the "OSHA Paper," because the Occupational Safety and Health Administration was, and is, actually using its estimates) was issued by two of the foremost epidemiologists studying environmental cancer, Richard Doll and Richard Peto. [22] Their paper is ruthless in its withering scorn. The OSHA estimates, report Doll and Peto "were so grossly in error that no argument based on them, even loosely, should be taken seriously." They point out that the risk estimates are more than ten times too high. And finally they declare that it seems likely that whoever wrote the OSHA paper did so for "political, rather than for scientific, purposes. . . . We would suggest that the OSHA paper should not be cited nor used as if it were."

In their analysis, prepared for the international world of cancer epidemiology, the U.S. health agencies have been charged with fabricating a politically motivated document, and scientists everywhere in the world have been warned that the "OSHA Paper" should be treated as a contaminant of the scientific literature.

All of this reaction has had little effect on U.S. government agencies, although the EPA now uses the figure of 40,000 for future cancer-caused deaths from inhaling asbestos, rather than the discredited two million OSHA figure. There are no data to substantiate either figure.

That there will be some cancer deaths from breathing asbestos is undenied, but no good is accomplished by using wildly exaggerated numbers. Moreover, the risk is mostly confined to smokers. For those known to be exposed to environmental asbestos who are also smokers, the risk of lung cancer is increased 50- to 90-fold. Finally, the degree of pulmonary disease risk depends upon the *kind* of asbestos involved.[23]

There are two different varieties of asbestos. The kind that occurs naturally in America and is mined and used here is the serpentine variety, a soft asbestos called chrysotile. It accounts for 95 percent of all asbestos used in the U.S. Its fibers are rather long and twisted and, unless present in extraordinarily heavy concentration, cannot penetrate into the lung alveoli and are rather easily expelled from the lungs. The other is the amphibole variety. It consists of a hard type of asbestos called crocodolite and one called amosite. Both are *very* dangerous.

Amphibole occurs only in South Africa. Its fibers are truly deadly; they are small enough to penetrate the air sacs, and once lodged in lung tissue, they are seldom eliminated. Because the hard amphibole type of asbestos is also extremely resistant to corrosion, it was imported from South Africa during World War II for use as insulation and fire protection around pipes in naval ships and other vessels built at that time. Under the conditions of wartime construction, proper worker protection was often lacking and it is these men that are now suffering from exposure to the most dangerous type of asbestos. They deserve to be compensated. The amphibole type of asbestos was also used until 1956 in the filters of Kent cigarettes.[24]

Asbestosis and mesothelioma are generally caused by breathing fibers of crocodolite. The soft-fibered chrysotile is generally benign. This is amply illustrated by the lack of asbestosis and lung cancer among Canadian asbestos miners and their families. Similarly, near San Francisco, California, there exists about 16 square miles of bare rock containing 50 percent chrysotile asbestos. Although the local people have been drinking chrysotile-rich water and breathing chrysotile-rich air for lifetimes, there is no heightened lung cancer incidence and certainly no cancer epidemic in that area of California.

Why, then, require removal of chrysotile asbestos from school buildings? Breathing *any* dust—baking flour, silica, dirt, coal dust—in excess could lead to pulmonary problems or disease, but chrysotile asbestos is not, of itself, very dangerous.

School rooms, measured before asbestos removal, reveal that the air usually contains about 0.00009 fibers per cubic centimeter; after removal, that number typically *rises* to 20 to 40 fibers per cubic centimeter—a 40,000-fold increase—and it may stay at that elevated level for years. Disturbing the asbestos material inevitably causes fibers to become airborne. It would be far better simply to ensure that the fibers stayed in place with a coating of good quality paint. But that is too simple, too inexpensive, compared to the estimated three to ten billion dollar cost for removal and replacement.[25]

And what will be used to replace the asbestos? Fiberglass? Rock wool? Both are much more carcinogenic than common chrysotile asbestos. But we can't expect OSHA or the EPA to know *that*. Our government agencies have to create crises and interfere in our lives to feel needed.

The Much Maligned PCBs[26]

PCBs—polychlorinated biphenyls, consist of a group of more than 200 chemical compounds. They range from light, oily fluids to heavy, greasy, or waxy substances. Their primary useful characteristic is that they are non-flammable. They are also very stable over a wide range of temperature and physical conditions, and they therefore have wide applicability as coolants and lubricants in transformers and other electrical equipment and as insulators. They do not occur in nature and were first prepared more than 100 years ago. Their commercial production and use began in 1929.

Since they markedly reduced fire hazards, PCBs found many uses as insulation in office buildings, factories, hospitals, and schools. But perhaps their most important application was to replace mineral oil, a flammable substance with a low flash point, in large electrical transformers and capacitors. So successful was this reduction in fire hazard that many city codes required the use of PCB, and banned transformers that had mineral oil as a coolant.

The property of stability, so important in the electrical applications, provided the opening wedge to the attack on and eventual banning of all uses of PCB. During the early years of its use, PCB was allowed, with proper permits, to be disposed of in rivers and waterways. PCB was therefore taken up in the bodies of fish, and eventually permeated the food chain. Although *no harm* has ever come from this, the appearance and spread of PCB in the environment was enough to raise alarm in the environmental organizations. Then an incident occurred that touched off a flurry of opposition.

In 1968, in Yusho, Japan, on the Island of Kyushu, 1,300 people became ill after eating rice contaminated with PCBs.[27] Instead of asking how the rice got mixed up with PCB and then rectifying the matter, the activist alarmists clamored for a total ban. The people who consumed the PCB-contaminated rice developed a skin rash, and many reported fatigue, nausea, swelling in the extremities, and liver disorders. In the years following this poisoning incident, it has become clear that PCB itself was not the cause of the adverse reaction. Rather, the fluid involved, only 50 percent of it PCB, had been in long use in air conditioning equipment and other heat exchangers. The high temperatures involved converted about half of the original material into quarterphenyls or polychlorinated dibenzofurans, which are very toxic. But PCB itself bore the blame, and this single incident was extrapolated in propaganda in the U.S., where such a contamination of food is highly unlikely.

The predictable result was a banning by the EPA, and no PCBs are in commercial use in the U.S. today. The other result is that utilities were required, at costs reaching into the millions of dollars, to reconvert their equipment and revert to the use of mineral oil or other insulating substances. The costs, of course, are paid by the electricity user, and once more we have sporadic transformer fires.

Finally, it is now known that PCBs do not remain stable in the environment for years on end. There are at least eight to ten strains of both aerobic and anaerobic bacteria that can and do degrade PCB to simple, harmless substances.[28] These bacteria are capable of reducing the concentration of PCB in water or soil by 60 to 65 percent every 20 days. So much for toxic, dangerous, "cancer-causing" PCBs.

How Toxic Is Dioxin?[29]

The question of the toxicity of dioxin is one of the more difficult and emotional issues in the whole field of hazardous chemicals—difficult because "dioxin" is a group of 75 different compounds of varied toxicity, of which 2,3,7,8-tetra-chlorodibenzo-p-dioxin (also called TCDD) is the most dangerous. Traces of this dioxin are found in some herbicides in common use and in many chlorinated organic compounds.

Many dioxins are detected in low concentration whenever organic material is burned, especially if the combustion is incomplete. Dioxins, therefore, are produced in forest fires, engine exhausts, and even in the materials emitted from volcanoes. How dangerous they may be is the subject of much controversy, both within the scientific community and in the public at large.[30]

Dioxin became an emotional issue when it was revealed to be a contaminating component of Agent Orange, used as a herbicide-defoliant during the Vietnam War. Extensive studies have been conducted on veterans who were exposed to Agent Orange compared to those who were not. There was no evidence discovered of damage to human health, but there was also no satisfactory answer to the question: How toxic is dioxin? Dioxin was also implicated in the contamination problems at Love Canal and at Times Beach.

Animal studies have not resolved the toxicity question; guinea pigs are very sensitive and show a high level of tumors and malignancies, as well as skin disorders, lung lesions, liver damage, blood disorders, loss of weight, and death after exposure to even small amounts. Hamsters, on the other hand, are very resistant; it takes a dose 5,000 times larger than the guinea pig dose to cause any adverse effect in hamsters. But people are neither guinea pigs nor hamsters, and the data on human exposures, while enormous, do not resolve the issue.

The established facts on the consequences of exposure to dioxin are these:

1. Dioxin is highly toxic to some animal species, of low toxicity to others.

2. Dioxin can be a potent animal carcinogen in guinea pigs.

3. There is no evidence that dioxin causes human cancer, spontaneous abortion, or birth defects.

4. No human has ever become chronically ill or died from dioxin exposure in the U.S.

5. The only proven human illness to result from dioxin exposure is chloracne—a severe skin rash that is curable with proper treatment—and possibly, a short-term nerve dysfunction.

6. The most heavily exposed population, 37,000 people of Seveso, Italy, who were dusted with one to four pounds of dioxin from an explosion at the ICMESA Chemical plant in 1976, suffered chloracne and some physical distress but no long-term adverse effect and no cancer.

7. Long-term studies (more than 30 years) on Monsanto workers exposed in 1949 to high levels of dioxin show no long-term effects.

Yet dioxin has been called "the most toxic chemical known to man," even though no deaths or serious harm to humans can be attributed to it. People believe that it is extremely dangerous, and that belief contributed to the hysteria that developed at Love Canal and at Times

Beach, when dioxin was detected in the environment of those two towns. In her scholarly and well documented book, *Toxic Terror*, Dr. Elizabeth Whelan, summarized the issue succinctly:

> There is nothing resembling a significant number of scientists and public health officials who feel that the dioxin and dioxin-containing herbicides have been responsible for the crimes with which they have been charged. To the television news programs, however, the scientific community's consensus is offered by a select group of the same "experts," over and over again.
>
> Rarely do we see coverage about the expert who finds, for example, that dioxin in soil samples does not pose much of a health threat to humans in the area. What we do see on television news programs are interviews with the few same scientists preaching horror stories and doomsday prophecies. During early 1983, almost every television report, documentary, and print story on the subject cited the University of Illinois' Dr. Samuel Epstein and Harvard's Dr. Matthew Meselson. Epstein, in particular, has frequently been quoted in absolute terms when the data on which he bases his statements are not accepted by the scientific community, such as this excerpt from the *Washington Post*: "The evidence is overwhelming that dioxin is carcinogenic in humans." The news media want sensationalism, and they know where they can get it.

As Joan Beck of *The Chicago Tribune* astutely wrote in her column of June 30, 1983: "Newspaper editors and broadcasters, who help set the national agenda by what they choose to report, have hyped the dioxin danger, made it more dramatic by their choice of human interest stories, ignored much of the scientific evidence and used quotes from some scientists whose conclusions weren't justified by their research."

Finally, it is the presence of minute traces (parts per billion or even parts per trillion) of dioxin that has caused so many waste disposal sites to be marked for cleanup under the "Superfund." Of approximately 1,000 sites now on the Superfund National Priorities List, only one dozen have been cleaned up at a cost, so far, of *nine billion dollars*. The average cleanup cost for each site is estimated to be at least $12 to

$15 million, with some going as high as $100 million. Reasonable estimates for total cleanup of all sites range from *one to ten trillion dollars*. Is the public health risk really this great?

Unfortunately, the public is unaware of these costs and their implications for short-changing other health problems, and of the potential implications for the economic vitality of America. [31]

Part Three

ISSUES
NUCLEAR

Chapter 8

RADIATION AROUND US

FOR ALL THOSE who do not like radioactivity, the Earth is no place to live. [1]

The simple fact is we inhabit a radioactive world, always have, and always will. Our bodies receive the impact of about 15,000 radioactive particles per second—that's 500 billion per year and 40 trillion in a lifetime. We don't feel them or suffer any apparent ill effect from this constant bombardment.

We have no human sense to detect radioactivity. No sight, sound, or smell reveals it. Radiation has been something like magnetism or gravity or molecules—unknown or at least not understood until instruments were developed that measure the phenomenon with incredible accuracy.

Indeed, one of the difficult aspects of the radiation phobia is that our ability to measure radioactivity has become so accurate and precise that it is now possible to detect the scintillation of a single atom. Unbelievably small amounts are measurable; for example, one part per billion is easily counted.

How much, or rather how little, is that? How can we visualize one part per billion? One way is by analogy: One part per billion (called a nanocurie) is equivalent to one drop of vermouth in five carloads of gin. Now that is a very dry martini.

95

Or, look at it another way: There are now about five billion people living on this planet. Therefore, one family of five persons represents one part per billion of the entire human population.

What about radioactivity at the level of one part per trillion? This unit is referred to as a picocurie (pCi) and is 1,000 times less than a nanocurie (nCi). It would be analogous to one drop of vermouth in 5,000 carloads of gin!

When clouds containing radioactivity from the Chernobyl accident in the U.S.S.R. in April 1986 reached the West Coast of the United States, the popular press was full of dire warnings about possible fallout, even reporting how many picocuries had been measured in the clouds. But nowhere did reporters explain that a pCi is one part in a trillion. A person would have to drink 63,000 gallons of rainwater, all at once, to receive as much radioactive iodine from the fallout as a patient receives in a diagnostic test for thyroid problems. A formidable task. [2]

There is radioactivity everywhere, in the ground, in sand and stone and clay. In the words of Walter Marshall (Lord Marshall of Goring), who served for years as head of Great Britain's Atomic Energy Council and is now director of the Central Electricity Generating Board: [3]

> In my own country, the United Kingdom, I like to point out that the average Englishman's garden occupies one tenth of an acre. By digging down one metre, we can extract six kilograms of thorium, two kilograms of uranium, and 7,000 kilograms of potassium, all of them radioactive. In a sense, all of that is radioactive waste, not man-made, but the residue left over when God created the planet.

There is plenty of radioactivity in the upper levels of the earth's crust, but there's more inside. It is the heat of radioactive decay that helps to keep the earth's core molten and provides warmth from inside that contributes to Earth's habitability. It is the heat of radioactive decay that provides much of the driving force for movement of the Earth's tectonic plates. This in turn accounts for the size and shape of continents and contributes to mountain building, to earthquakes, and to volcanic eruptions.

There is radioactivity in water and in the atmosphere. In all, about 70 different radioactive elements occur in our natural environment. The energy that reaches Earth from the Sun includes cosmic rays that strike molecules in the upper atmosphere and produce the isotopes Carbon-14 and Potassium-40, both of them radioactive and found in the bodies of all living things.

Of the total radiation that is received on average by each American every year, 82 percent comes from natural sources. Only 18 percent is man-made.[4] Of the natural radioactivity, a little more than half, 55 percent, is from radon; 8 percent is from cosmic sources and solar flares; another 8 percent is from terrestrial sources, mainly uranium and thorium, and 11 percent comes from internal Potassium-40. The remaining 18 percent that is man-made consists of medical X-rays, which account for 11 percent; nuclear medicine, 4 percent; consumer products, such as smoke detectors, tobacco, and ceramics, etc., 3 percent, and all other sources about 1 percent. The latter figure, 1 percent, includes the entire nuclear energy industry, which contributes no more than 0.1 percent of our entire radiation exposure.

Two points should be emphasized. First, radioactivity is radioactivity, whether made by humans or found in nature. Alpha particles, for example, consist of two protons and two neutrons. They are positively charged and strongly ionizing—regardless of their origin. Beta rays are electrons, no matter where or what they come from. Gamma rays are short electromagnetic rays; at low energy, they behave like X-rays. Alpha particles can be easily blocked. They do not penetrate through a sheet of paper, whereas gamma radiation penetrates tissues readily.

I emphasize the nature of alpha, beta, and gamma radiation, *regardless of source*, because some anti-nuclear activists have recently adopted the curious attitude—a position amounting to a strange mental ambivalence—that somehow man-made radiation is different from and, therefore, more dangerous than the benign radiation of nature. They are wrong.

Natural radiation also includes cosmic rays, which are a mixture of high energy photons and particles, mainly protons and electrons, with a smaller number of helium nuclei and metallic nuclei.[5] Cosmic rays originate both in space and in the Sun. They are abundant in solar flares and can cause brilliant auroras when they collide with oxygen or nitrogen in the upper atmosphere. Collision with oxygen produces red or green colors and interaction with nitrogen causes blue or violet auroras. Finally, ultraviolet rays have wave lengths shorter than visible light. They are a component of sunlight and are also produced in tanning parlors. The ultraviolet rays from these two sources are indistinguishable and the effects on human skin are the same.

The second point to emphasize is this: With all this radiation bombarding us from every direction, why aren't we, all of us, stricken with cancer? The reason is that, although exposure to very high levels of radiation can result in the type of cellular damage that leads to growth of a cancer, the situation is by no means clear with respect to low level exposures, even when they are chronic. The risk appears to be very small, indeed, and evidence is accumulating that low levels of radiation may be either harmless or a positive benefit! So radical a statement requires thorough examination.

For one thing, cells, which evolved from Day One in a radiation-rich environment, have an incredible ability to repair themselves from moderate radiation damage. This has been especially well studied in plant tissues and lower organisms. Additionally, most direct strikes from radioactive particles result in dead cells, not injured ones, and dead cells do not grow to produce cancers. It takes a very special kind of non-lethal damage for a cell to be genetically damaged or to become cancerous. The exact nature of this damage is unknown, as is the exact amount and kind of radioactivity that may cause it in humans or other species.

For another thing, the risk is very small. Let's compare the odds to those of a lottery. Of course, it's possible that any person who buys a lottery ticket may win the jackpot, but the reality is that most do not. In the case of natural radioactivity, the chance that any one of the 40 trillion particles that strike every person over a lifetime will cause a cancer or a genetic effect is one in 50 quadrillion. That's one in 50 million billion, or one in 50,000,000,000,000,000.[6] Pretty good odds—for no effect at all. And most people do not worry about natural radioactivity.

Even so, we know that a high enough exposure can cause cancer. So, how much is high enough? We generally speak in average exposures, but the amount of natural, background radiation varies greatly from place to place. In the United States, the average annual natural or background radioactivity is about 300 to 350 millirems, but the range is great; it may be as low as 60 millirems or as high as 600. A millirem is one-thousandth of a rem, which stands for Roentgen Equivalent Man. This unit represents the actual ionizing effect on the human body. One millirem would be the dose from one year of watching color TV for a few hours per day. For each one millirem of radiation we receive, it is calculated that our risk of dying from cancer is increased by about one chance in eight to ten million. Put another way: One millirem is equivalent to being struck by about seven billion particles of radiation. A Curie equates to 37 billion disintegrations per second, which is the activity of one gram of radium.

Extensive research has established that it takes exposures well in excess of 100,000 millirems for a detectable effect. Cancer will result in half of the cases at exposures of 400,000 millirems. As a result of the Three Mile Island nuclear power plant accident, the surrounding population received an additional radiation exposure of 1.2 millirems. Compare this to the natural background of:

- 30 millirems per year from cosmic rays.
- 20 millirems per year from the ground.
- 10 millirems per year from building materials (except for such buildings as Grand Central Station in New York or the Capitol building in Washington, D.C., where the granite or marble gives exposures in excess of 100 millirems annually).
- 25 millirems per year from internal Potassium-40.
- 80 millirems per year from medical procedures.
- 180 millirems or more from radon.

The totals are about 360 millirems per year for every American. In the Rocky Mountain states, where there is a higher uranium-thorium concentration in the soil and the altitude means more exposure to cosmic rays, the natural radiation is about twice the average, and in Florida it is 15 percent below.

In some places, the natural background radiation reaches abnormally high concentrations. Hot springs and mineral water resorts usually have elevated amounts of radioactivity. For example, the "wondrous waters" of the English city of Bath[7] have a radon content of 1,730 pCi per liter; recall that the EPA has set a level for homes of 4 pCi per liter, above which remedial action should be taken. The radon in natural gas at Bath is 33,650 pCi per liter. The Romans built a temple there in 43 A.D. and dedicated it to the Goddess of Wisdom and Health, and in 1742, the Royal National Hospital for rheumatic diseases was established there. It is still a premier research center for the study of rheumatism. People flock to Bath and to other hot spring spas, all of them with elevated radioactivity, for their reputed beneficial health effects. There is no proof that the radiation makes people feel better, but there is also no evidence that it has any ill effect on the visitors who both bathe or soak in the springs and drink the waters. It is unfortunate that most of the information about the health benefits of hot springs is anecdotal, for here is a wonderful opportunity to study both the patients (visitors) and the resident population, not only at Bath but also at Baden Baden; Warm Springs, Georgia; White Springs, Virginia; and multitudes of other resorts.

Even more, one wonders why good, thorough, modern studies have not been conducted on the resident populations in Cochin-Ernakulum in the state Kerala on the southwestern coast of India, where the thorium-bearing soils give annual exposures of up to 16,000 millirems per year, and on people living in several areas of Brazil. Many seacoast beaches in northeastern Brazil are composed of black mineral sands called Monagite, noted for its high radiation levels. Visitors flock to these beaches by the thousands for their reputed health benefits. Exposures on the black sands there are estimated to exceed 500 millirems per year. Yet radiation experts in this country consider these populations to be "too small to permit meaningful epidemiologic investigations. . . ."[8]

And then there are the two extraordinary regions of high natural radiation, one in Africa and the other in Brazil. In Gabon, West Africa, near a place called Oklo, where there is now a uranium mine, the concentration of the fissionable isotope U-235 was once so high that 1.8 billion years ago a natural chain reaction set in. Nature produced a nuclear fission "reactor" that "operated" or sustained criticality for a period of one million years. Tons of uranium were burned and both plutonium and other typical fission reactor isotopes (transuranics) were produced. Even though the reactor area has been subject to rainfall and other weathering agents, the plutonium and fission isotopes have migrated only a few meters from the place of their production. This natural nuclear reactor has been thoroughly studied.

Not so with the Brazilian area called Morro do Ferro, a weathered mound 250 meters tall that is formed of an ore body containing an estimated 30,000 metric tons of thorium and 100,000 metric tons of rare earths. The radiation level is one to two mRoentgens per hour over an area of 30,000 square meters. The mound supports both animal and plant life. So high is the absorbed radioactivity in the vegetation that photographs can be taken—autoradiographs—showing the plants truly glowing in the dark.

A colony of rats occupies burrows in the mound. Measurements show that they breathe an atmosphere containing radon at levels up to 100 pCi per milliliter! (100,000 pCi/liter). The radiation dose to the rats' bronchial epithelium is estimated to be between 3,000 and 30,000 rems per year, roughly three times the concentration that should produce tumors or other radiation effects. Fourteen rats were trapped and autopsied, and no abnormalities were found. Yet the investigator who made these measurements commented, "This is of little significance, since the Morro do Ferro is a relatively small area."[9]

It also seems likely that radiation scientists are loath to believe that life exists—plant, animal, and human—in regions where the background natural radiation is abnormally high and yet suffer no apparent ill-effect, even with exposures exceeding 10,000 millirems per year, the generally accepted cutoff between low-level and high-level radiation. I'll have more on this interesting topic after we consider two well known radioactive elements, radium and radon.

Of course radiation is dangerous, and that includes natural radioactivity. The degree of danger depends on the dose—the amount, kind, and duration of the exposure—and on the knowledge of how to handle radioactivity. The latter is of great importance. It can be said with confidence that, because of extensive research programs pursued since the 1940s, more is known about the effects of ionizing radiation than about the consequences of exposure to any of the many toxic substances that exist in nature or have been introduced into the environment.

From its discovery up to the 1940s, radium was applied to a number of commercial products. Using radioluminescent paint on the numbers on the faces of watches, clocks, and other instruments so they could be read in the dark was a widespread practice. Less well known was a similar application—on the lid and handles of the chamber pot, before the days of indoor plumbing and electric lights in the home! About two pounds of radium were extracted from the ground and put in commercial or medical use during the first 50 years of its availability. Worldwide, at least 100 people died from its improper use or mishandling. Since 1942, various atomic energy programs have produced the radioactive equivalent of many tons of radium. But because of greater knowledge and understanding, not one human death has resulted from exposure or internal deposition of a wide variety of artificially produced radio-nuclides.[10]

Of all the naturally occurring radioactive materials, none has received more public attention recently than radon. It is believed that this widespread element in nature is responsible for between 5,000 to 30,000 deaths from lung cancer annually in the United States. Is this so, and is it a new threat? In a sense, yes. I'll return to the question shortly.

The history of our knowledge of radon started in the Erz Mountains (between Germany and Czechoslovakia) in the sixteenth century. In a book about mining, it was reported that most men who worked the metal mines eventually died from "mountain disease," a respiratory illness. It was not until 1879 that it was recognized as lung cancer.[11]

After the discovery of radioactivity and the identification of radon as a breakdown product of radium, it was found that the Erz Mountain mines had exceptionally high levels of radon. A connection between radon and lung cancer was suspected but not established until the 1950s, when studies were undertaken of U.S. uranium miners. The

U.S. mines provided a far healthier work environment than those in the Erz Mountains, but the levels of radon were similar. The study results showed conclusively that where radon concentrations were greatest, so also were the number of cases of lung cancer—and where radon levels were lowest, so was the rate of lung cancers. Further studies of the Czech miners confirmed the U.S. results, so that by 1976, radon-induced lung cancer became the best quantified of all health effects of radiation.

Improved ventilation to remove the radon from mines has essentially eliminated the problem for miners, but now it has become clear that radon alone is not the culprit. Smoking, particularly cigarette smoking, now appears to be an important triggering agent. Moreover, at the Austrian mine at Joachinosthal, A. Pirchman reported in the *American Journal of Cancer*, 1932, that there were no lung cancers in any of the working miners—only among the "pensioners," two-thirds of whom died of lung cancer. The average life expectancy then was 55 years; the miners lived longer and retired at 65![12] The moral is, if you worked the mines and breathed radon, you got lung cancer—*but only after you outlived the general population*.

Now, let's take a closer look at radon.[13]

Remember, radon is a gas. Inert, chemically neutral, and radioactive, it appears in the natural decay chain of uranium. There are 14 different steps in this chain, and the important immediate precursor to radon is the radioactive element, radium, itself a decay product of uranium.

Some atoms of radium undergo a radioactive process called "alpha decay," meaning that the nucleus of these atoms spontaneously eject a cluster of nuclear particles consisting of two neutrons and two protons bound together. This is the alpha particle. It is the loss of the two protons that converts radium (Atomic Number 88) to radon (Atomic Number 86). Alpha-emitting substances are not dangerous unless they get inside the body, and they are not "penetrating"—that is, they can be blocked by barriers. Even a sheet of paper is sufficient.

So, the process that produces radon starts with uranium. Uranium is ubiquitous, and since it is widespread throughout the earth, radon gas can appear anywhere. Typically, about six atoms per second from every square inch of soil come bubbling up through the ground, where they dissipate into the atmosphere. At least, that is what happens in nature.

When people build homes and other structures, these natural radio-active processes in the ground beneath are in no way affected. The only difference is that when radon gas seeps to the surface under a home, it moves into and through the construction. Radon enters buildings through the foundation, through cracks, crevices, and fissures, and through the freshwater supply. It is then trapped indoors for some time.

In an average home, the normal radon level may be as much as ten times what it is outdoors—sometimes 100 times. How does the trapped radon gas get out of houses and other buildings? Essentially, the same way it came in—through cracks and fissures, except that this time the openings are above ground, around windows and doors, and through walls and roofs. In old-fashioned homes, minute openings and spaces around the doors, windows, and elsewhere permit a ventilation rate, or exchange of atmosphere, once or twice per hour, and radon accumulation is usually not a problem. But in a modern, tightly sealed, energy-conserving home, this ventilation rate is reduced to about one exchange of the atmosphere per day.

The rate of radon entering the energy-efficient home from the ground beneath is not changed, but the rate of leaving is. Therefore, the radon is trapped longer and builds up inside. *Sealing up a home for the purpose of energy conservation inevitably leads to higher levels of indoor radon.* Is this bad? Yes. That, too, needs explanation.

The focus of concern about the hazard of indoor radiation is on radon, but it is not the gas itself that is the problem. Rather, it is the further radioactive breakdown of radon leading to the formation of what are called "radon daughters" that causes trouble. Radon itself radiates only weakly, and its half-life is 3.82 days. Since it is inert, it does not react chemically in the body, and when inhaled, radon gas will be exhaled again. But if radon daughters are inhaled, the situation is quite different. They are solid particles, have short half-lives, emit alpha particles or beta particles, and are intensely radioactive. More-over, radon daughters tend to adhere to dust particles, which easily become airborne and thus inhaled. They also adhere to smoke particles. That's one reason "passive" smoking—that is, breathing smoke in a closed atmosphere—is so dangerous. Carried to the lungs, the radon daughters will likely stick to the mucous membrane and bombard the sensitive tissue with intense radioactivity. This is what may cause lung cancer.

Radon daughters can pile up in rooms that are not well ventilated. Some typical radon daughters are:

- Polonium-218, half-life 3.05 minutes, an alpha emitter.
- Bismuth-214, half-life 19.7 minutes, a beta emitter (electron).
- Lead-214, half-life 26.8 minutes, beta emitter.

Let's use Bismuth-214 as an example. In indoor air that has accumulated radon daughters for three minutes (three-minute air), Bismuth-214 will contribute 0.5 percent of the total radioactive particle energy; it will contribute four percent in ten-minute air and 38 percent in non-circulating air.

At a ventilation rate of one or two times per hour (in most American homes), the radon accumulation is approximately one picocurie per liter of air (to repeat: one picocurie is one part in a trillion). This translates to an exposure of roughly 100 millirems per year, about one-third of the average annual radiation exposure and well within the 500-millirem maximum recommended for the population as a whole by the Environmental Protection Agency.

Two things, however, can increase this average exposure to radon: living in an energy-efficient home and living in an area where the natural concentration of uranium is high. Most granitic soils contain larger than normal amounts of uranium; in parts of New England, for example, radon exposures tend to be elevated. The geological formation best known for its high uranium-radon levels is the Reading Prong, which extends roughly from Reading, Allentown, and Easton, Pennsylvania, through Morristown, New Jersey, and into New York State. Some homes built on this formation have been found to have 1,000 times the average radon level, and dozens have been found with levels hundreds of times the average. To date, the highest radon level measure is in a home in Boyertown, Pennsylvania—2,500 times the average![14]

The naturally occurring outdoor radon, to which every American is exposed to some degree, might lead to lung cancer. In a population the size of the United States, approximately 10,000 cases per year are attributed to this source. Energy conservation, as urged by the U.S. government, will approximately double this number. Tobacco smoke further increases the cancer danger of this exposure. Perhaps the fuel-saving brought about by tightly sealing up one's domicile is worth the slight additional risk of lung cancer, but, if so, the decision should be made by the homeowner, by individual citizens knowledgeable about the consequences of their acts—not by a government enforcing strict energy codes or by utilities offering attractive incentives to "leakproof" one's residence. The choice of taking a risk should be left to the person involved, but he should have sufficient and accurate information to make an informed decision.

Although the facts about the increased risks of radon/radon daughter buildup in energy-efficient homes have been known since the late 1970s, the EPA issued no warnings and didn't release its long expected guide on indoor radon concentration until August 1986. What took the agency so long? Is energy conservation so overwhelmingly important that it transcends public health problems?

The EPA guide says nothing about the dangers of sealed up buildings. Instead, it calls for remedial action to be taken whenever the indoor radon level rises above four picocuries per liter of air (equivalent to roughly 400 millirems exposure per year). According to EPA estimates, this level is already exceeded by some 11 million homes, involving more than 26 million people in the United States. Ironically, the four picocuries per liter of air is 40 times higher than the very strict limit that applies to the nuclear industry! Why should stricter limits apply to the workplace, where perhaps an adult family member spends, say, one-third of each day, than to the domestic residence, where the entire family, including infants and children, spends two-thirds or more of each day?

One explanation for this regulatory absurdity is that whereas the

EPA regulates radiation hazards in homes, the Nuclear Regulatory Commission (NRC) regulates radiation hazards in nuclear facilities. The NRC sets very strict and very low limits for the nuclear industry; indeed, if the *de minimus* rule adopted were to be enforced by the NRC, as urged by environmental activists, most natural, outside air would be illegal.

Two recent episodes involving radiation exposure should be remarked upon. First, there was the tragic accident at the Chernobyl plant in Russia. *Outside* the evacuation zone, the radiation exposure to Soviet citizens was equivalent to the exposure New England citizens get *every year* from living in their radon-rich homes for about eight months.

Second, in 1984, a federal judge in Utah awarded $2.6 million damages to ten plaintiffs whose radiation exposures from atmospheric bomb tests between 1961 and 1962 did not exceed 500 millirems per year. This is far less than the exposures in many energy-efficient homes; some in New England exceed it by factors of ten or more. In delivering his verdict, Federal Judge Bruce S. Jenkins made a statement that should command the attention of both governmental agencies and the news media.[15] He said the government was negligent in its "failure to adequately warn plaintiffs . . . of known or foreseen long-range biological consequences" of its actions, and, in addition, of failure to "adequately and continuously inform individuals of well-known and inexpensive methods to prevent or mitigate the effects of inhaled radioactive particles."

Where are the government-issued warnings about radon in energy-efficient homes? Our government has actively promoted energy-efficient homes with everything from do-it-yourself literature to tax breaks for insulating your home. Where has the press been? Aiding and abetting the government.

Perhaps the time has come to let in some fresh air, to improve home ventilation by opening up the windows, even at the cost of higher energy consumption. Perhaps it's not too much to expect that the cause of common sense and public health could be served by a truly free press—freed from the silly notion that energy conservation is a good that transcends all and freed from the mindless assumption that radon trapped in a sealed house won't hurt you while radon seeping from uranium mine tailings (where nobody lives) will. It's all the same radiation. We should open the windows and let the fresh air in—and the radon out.

Or, better yet, let's stop building airtight homes and buildings that not only develop radon accumulation problems but also suffer from another very modern phenomenon, "indoor air pollution." So bad is the poorly ventilated indoor air in some newly constructed energy-efficient buildings that an entirely new problem has emerged, the Sick Building Syndrome.

Increasingly, the occupants and workers in newly built energy-conserving buildings are complaining of adverse health effects. Respiratory illnesses, allergies, headaches, and skin problems appear to be common, and adequate ventilation, reduced by energy-conserving construction, is becoming recognized as a serious problem. Few conclusive studies have been conducted, but one is instructive. It involves the health of Army recruits living in groups of 100 to 250 men in new, tightly sealed barracks with forced ventilation, compared to other groups of men assigned to old barracks. [16]

Four Army training centers, located in the southeastern and south-central United States, were included. Recently constructed, well-insulated, mechanically ventilated quarters were paired with old, World War II-vintage barracks. The study covered different groups of trainees over a 47-month period from October 1, 1982, to September 1, 1986. It was found that for the entire period the risk of respiratory illness was increased in the modern barracks by 45 percent or more at each of the four centers. During epidemic periods, the relative risk of respiratory disease in the modern barracks reached 100 percent. The conclusion is that "in tight buildings with closed ventilation systems, airborne pathogens are not only re-circulated and concentrated but also efficiently dispersed through indoor living spaces, while in 'leaky' buildings, airborne-transmitted agents are diluted by fresh outdoor air and relatively quickly exhausted from indoor spaces." So much for energy-efficient homes and buildings.

These paired modern problems of indoor radon and indoor air pollution, amounting now to a public health issue for all Americans, have been brought about by environmental zealots who insist that conservation is the preferred, if not the only, way to deal with assuring sufficient energy. If the same amount of devotion and effort had been directed toward building new electricity generating plants as has been wasted on tightly sealing our buildings, we would have a healthier population, as well as enough electricity to heat (and cool) structures in a clean, safe, and healthy manner—without respiratory problems. Energy conservation, however noble it may seem, is no more a "source" of energy than money under the mattress is a "source" of income.

Now it is time to return to the question: How harmful is exposure to low levels of radiation; that is, levels below 10,000 millirems per year? We've seen examples of apparently healthy populations living in areas of exceedingly high natural radiation. What about living with elevated levels of radon? How hazardous is it? Fortunately, there are now available extensive data from very recent investigations, which may cause some fundamental change in our attitude toward and understanding of chronic exposure to low-level radioactivity. Here we must introduce the concept of Hormesis.

Hormesis

A very long time ago, in the sixteenth century, a German physician known as Paracelsus (Theophrastus Bombastus von Hohenheim) developed a proposition that has become a fundamental principle of toxicology.

"What is it that is not poison?" he wrote. "All things are poison and none without poison. Only the dose determines that a thing is not poison."[17]

This is the concept of Hormesis. The validity of this principle has been confirmed over and over again. Even seemingly benign or necessary substances, such as water, can be toxic if taken in large enough doses. In 1979, a man in Germany died because he drank 17 liters of water within a very short time. The immediate cause of death was cerebral edema and electrolytic disturbance due to excess water.

This simple, common-sense principle, "the dose is the poison," also holds true for radiation. Clearly high doses of radiation can cause injury or death; conversely, low doses (as those from natural radioactivity) are, for all practical purposes, harmless. At what level of exposure does radioactivity become a "poison"?

Extensive research has established that exposures above 10,000 rems (10 million millirems) are lethal. Exposures of 300 rems (300,000 millirems) are fatal for roughly half of those who are exposed. Radiation injury is likely at exposures from 100 rems to 300 rems, but no deleterious reactions have been found at levels below 100 rems (100,000 millirems).[18]

Recall that the average exposure to natural background radiation in the U.S. is 350 millirems. Empirically, therefore, on the basis of many observations, measurements, and experiments, it would seem that there is a threshold for damaging radiation below which no adverse effects are found, and that threshold is about 100,000 millirems. But there is great argument about this, with most scientists accepting the "linear hypothesis," which holds that some effect occurs, decreasing toward zero, that is perhaps not detected nor measurable but can be calculated by extrapolating downward from effects at high level exposure.

A few scientists (and many laymen) go further and believe that *no* level of radiation is safe. We might note, in passing, that the linear hypothesis does not explain the absence of any detectable effect from living in a radioactive world. Since the radiation science community has not settled on the threshold or linear hypothesis, let us consider the evidence.

Early in the Manhattan District days (1943), radiation scientists were concerned about the toxicity of uranium. They exposed a colony of rats to an atmosphere laden with uranium dust with another colony breathing fresh air as a control. Although the researchers expected the high level of uranium to be fatal, the experimental rats lived out their normal life span and outlived the control rats. Moreover, they appeared healthier than the control rats and had more offspring. They developed no tumors. Most radiation scientists today consider this experiment flawed and dismiss the result as an anomaly.[19]

But similar results keep accumulating. In 1980, Professor T. D. Luckey published the conclusions from 1,239 separate studies of many investigators involving living things from cell cultures and bacteria to plants (800 references) and animals (200 references) of many different species exposed to varying amounts of ionizing radiation of all types. He reports that the results are consistent: There is a threshold or cutoff point below which ionizing radiation is either harmless or beneficial. Luckey concluded that ionizing radiation is generally stimulating in low doses; that low doses give accelerated development, increased resistance to disease, greater reproductivity, and longer life span; that low doses do not give proportionate harmful effects; that radiation is less dangerous in low doses than usually believed; and that chronic irradiation in doses slightly above ambient may be beneficial for both animals and plants. [20]

Still, many radiation scientists are reluctant to accept these findings as applicable to humans. Experiments on humans are out of the question, but the extensive data relating radon exposure to human lung cancer provide a unique opportunity to compare lung cancer rates among populations living in areas with different amounts of radon naturally present. The results are interesting:

- In Cornwall, England, radon exposures are 100 times larger than the average British exposure, but there is no increased incidence of lung cancer.
- Cumberland County, Pennsylvania, has nine times the average U.S. radon exposure but is well below the average U.S. lung cancer rate.
- In Finland, where indoor radon levels average 2.5 picocuries per liter (2.5 times the world average), the lung cancer incidence among Finnish women is only 70 percent of that of other industrialized countries.

Similar data are available for Colorado and other high mountain states with more than average natural radioactivity. Recently, in 1987, a group of Austrian scientists presented the results of a carefully documented epidemiological study of various types of cancer in the

United States (at the Fourth International Symposium on Natural Radiation Environment).[21] They concluded that when the background radiation was between 350 and 500 millirems per year, the smallest number of cancers were found.

Professor B. L. Cohen of the University of Pittsburgh, analyzing 39,000 measurements of radon exposures versus lung cancer in 411 U.S. counties, has found the correlation to be negative at low levels— the more radon, the less lung cancer! His data are corrected for housing differences in cities versus rural areas and for cigarette smoking.[22]

Additional evidence for Hormesis or for a threshold below which adverse effects are lacking comes from many careful modern studies that fail to find the results predicted if one extrapolates downward from high level exposures. These include studies of chromosome damage by radiation in human white blood cells, malignancy due to radiation in mouse embryo cells, cancer incidence in mice exposed to various doses of gamma rays, cancer incidence in mice injected with radioactive material, leukemia rates in survivors of Hiroshima, and data on watch dial painters exposed to radium.

Whether one chooses to believe that exposure to low level radiation can be beneficial, we can say with confidence that assuming a linear relationship (rather than a threshold) will overestimate the possible damage—and the public prefers to believe the worst.

With exposure to low levels of radiation—below 10,000 millirems—we have a situation in which belief can override evidence. This is a mental phenomenon that is not unknown. For centuries, even well educated persons believed that, among humans, men had one less rib than women because of the biblical story that God created Eve from Adam's rib. This belief persisted, despite the availability of proof to the contrary: Count the ribs in skeletons. There is nothing in our philosophy, Horatio, that is true or false—but thinking makes it so.

So it is with radiation.

Chapter 9

NUCLEAR MEDICINE

THE NUCLEAR AGE began July 16, 1945, when the Trinity shot shattered the early morning calm of White Sands, New Mexico. With that explosion, scientists and engineers demonstrated how much they had learned about the forces that bind the atom, and our world was changed forever.

This phenomenon of the twentieth century is comparable in importance to man's discovery of fire. At the time of Trinity—or even when the "Atoms for Peace Program" was announced by President Eisenhower in 1953—no one could have predicted the enormous benefits that would derive from nuclear science. Prominent among these are the advances in medicine that have occurred over the last few decades. Nothing has been more decisive or made a more lasting impact than the application of nuclear knowledge in medical diagnosis and therapy.[1] In the United States alone, there are now about ten million nuclear-based diagnostic and 30,000 therapeutic procedures performed annually.[2] No modern hospital or medical school is without a department of nuclear medicine.

Roughly, the field of nuclear medicine divides into two areas, one utilizing instruments and isotopes to detect health problems and the other using radiopharmaceuticals to treat them.[3] With sophisticated imaging instruments that can "see" and record the radiation from tiny amounts of isotopes, a physician can obtain detailed pictures of any part of the human body. These procedures permit looking deeply into the body, without the risk of exploratory surgery and without pain, to observe the delicate functions of internal organs and detect or treat disease in its early stages. Tumors, for example, can be identified months before they are detectable by surgery or any other means.

An example of the efficiency of these techniques involves use of the radioactive element, Technetium-99, to examine the spleen for possible damage. Impact accidents and falls often lead to spleen rupture and internal bleeding, which, if undetected, can be fatal, since the spleen itself is a virtual reservoir of blood. Aside from monitoring blood pressure, which can fall for many reasons, including trauma, exploratory surgery used to be the only sure way of determining whether there was injury to the spleen. Now, with a simple injection of Technetium-99 into the bloodstream, blood flow into and from the spleen can be observed. A gamma ray camera is used to scan the body; if the spleen is hemorrhaging, it will show the damage, and if not, surgery is not necessary. The whole procedure takes only a few minutes and does not require hospitalization.

An X-ray machine is the oldest instrument that exploits radiation. It is still the one used most for detecting bone fractures, gross problems of the skeleton, and dental caries. Infinitely improved in recent years, the modern X-ray instrument has great sensitivity and focusing ability so that exposures are minimal. The X-ray differs from a typical nuclear medicine procedure in that the X-radiation originates outside the body and is transmitted through the body to expose X-ray film. Only bone or other dense structures will block the very penetrating X-rays, so this procedure has little usefulness in detecting problems in soft tissue.

In nuclear scanning techniques, a small amount of radioactive substance is injected into the bloodstream, usually through a vein in the arm. The movement of the radioactive material through the circulatory system or its eventual absorption in any organ or gland can readily be detected by the proper recording device, located outside the body. Typically, the radioactive material is a gamma emitter, and the recorder-counter is a gamma camera.

Originally, the gamma camera was called a "scintillation counter" because it incorporates a crystal that converts the radiation into light energy that scintillates or "flashes" whenever hit by a particle of gamma radiation. With photomultipliers to amplify the signal, sensitivity to measure and record a single photon, and computer control and enhancement techniques, a picture of the affected area can be obtained that has great detail and clarity.

The various modern instruments—called Positron Emission Tomography (PET), Single Photon Emission Computed Tomography (SPECT), and Nuclear Magnetic Resonance Imaging (NMRI)—all make use of the tomography principle; that is, by focusing up or down, they obtain information from "slices" through the body, whereby a three-dimensional image can be built up. Although Nuclear Magnetic Resonance Imaging is the proper name for this process (magnetic resonance is a different physical phenomenon), the word, "nuclear," is generally dropped so as not to offend the sensitivities of emotional patients. Both PET and SPECT are capable of making biochemical processes visible, while NMRI pictures reveal structure in great detail. All of these instruments operate without pain to the patient and are making "exploratory" surgery obsolete, a thing of the past.

The most commonly used radionuclide for diagnostic procedures is Technetium-99. This element does not occur in nature; it is produced in a nuclear reactor. It is used in most hospitals for more than 90 percent of all nuclear procedures; it is low in power, with a short half-life of about six hours, and it provides good pictures from most parts of the body. Technetium-99 is used for brain scans and for studies of the lungs and liver.

Iodine-131 is used to diagnose problems of the thyroid, Xenon-133 for lung scanning, Thallium-201 for getting images of the heart, and Gallium-67 for various soft-tissue tumors. The gamma radiation from Cobalt-60 is also highly effective in killing cancerous cells without affecting the surrounding healthy tissue, and every year about half a million people in more than 70 countries are treated for cancer with 2,500 Cobalt-60 therapy machines. [4]

In addition to acting as tracers or markers, radioisotopes are also valuable for treating diseases, especially since the radiation they produce can kill the abnormal cells of cancer. Radioactive Phosphorus-32, for example, selectively locates in bone marrow, where its beta radiation destroys cancer cells without harming normal ones. Phosphorus-32 is also used in treating blood diseases.

Advances in the understanding of antibodies have led to another approach, one that utilizes a selected radionuclide and attaches it to a monoclonal antibody that will seek out and lodge in the targeted area, where the isotope can effectively deliver its radiation. This procedure has great value, because the monoclonal antibodies can "home in" on the affected area, no matter how small it might be. The body can therefore be swept clean of small metastases; this is not possible with surgery or with any other known technique.

Other treatment techniques utilize carriers like tiny glass or ceramic beads incorporating radioactive Yttrium-90, which, injected into the proper spot, will circulate, for example, in the liver until they lodge in the capillaries of a cancerous area. There they are trapped right where the radiation is needed. In early 1989, 53 patients were being treated with that experimental procedure, and they had reported relief from the terrible pain of liver cancer. There is also some indication of life extension.

The graduate nuclear program at the University of Missouri, utilizing its research nuclear reactor, is a leader in isotope research for medical applications.[5] In addition to the Yttrium beads that the university developed, it is pioneering the use of Samarian-153 and Rhenium-186 for relief of pain in cancer of the bone. Rhenium-186 is also being tagged to monoclonal antibodies for treatment of colon cancer and Palladium-103 for cancer of the prostate. Potassium-40 is being used for investigation of cystic fibrosis and Sodium-24 is being used for hypertension. Already examination of the role of Selenium in the diet, using tracer techniques, has shown that it has some protective effect against both pancreatic and colon cancer.

Nuclear medicine has to be the great unsung success story of the Nuclear Age. Perhaps the lack of recognition is just as well; if it maintains a low profile, the mindless zealots of the anti-nuclear movement might continue to ignore it, and lives will continue to be saved.

Closely related to the diagnostic and therapeutic function of nuclear medicine is the application of ionizing radiation for sterilizing medical materials and for disinfecting or disinfesting food and sewage.

Nearly every hospital now uses its Cobalt-60 source to sterilize a multitude of items from bandages and blankets to hypodermic needles and syringes, surgical supplies, transfusion sets, kidney transplantation kits, oxygenators, catheters, plastic labware, dialysis units, and more. Burn ointments and enzymes, eye ointment, cataract removal instruments, bone joints are all sterilized with radiation, as are infant bottles, corks, nipples, sanitary napkins, and tampons.

Consumer items, such as peat moss and goat hair, cannot be cleansed in any other way. (It was to kill the anthrax bacillus in goat hair that Australia installed the world's first gamma irradiator in the late 1940s.)[7] First-aid kits are also routinely radiation-treated. How many people, using a band-aid with full confidence in its sterility, appreciate that its safety is due to ionizing radiation? The beauty of using gamma radiation for everything from tongue depressors to contact lens solutions and milk cartons is that it has unique penetrating properties. This means that the material to be sterilized can first be packaged or bottled and sealed, then bombarded with gamma rays to kill off any microbes, spores, or disease organisms. There is no induced radiation and the contents remain sterile until the container is opened.

Patients who have undergone transplantation surgery must be treated with drugs that suppress the immune system, making them very vulnerable to infection. Their diet, therefore, consists of food sterilized by irradiation. So, also, is the food eaten by all astronauts in America's space program.[8] They have reported that the irradiated fare is infinitely more palatable and better tasting than food sterilized by any other method. This is not surprising, since about 40 years of research have gone into developing the techniques for irradiating food.

Gamma radiation, because it is so penetrating as well as ionizing, can disrupt cells, even when they exist as pathogens deep within other tissues—as, for example, the trichina worm, which commonly infests pork, or the bacterium salmonella, which may be found within the body cavity of chickens, in eggs, in other poultry, and in seafood. With the proper amount of exposure, these disease-causing organisms can be destroyed without affecting the quality or taste of the food. Indeed, there is no other procedure known that can safely rid an egg of salmonella. Likewise, invading agents from fungus spores to insects and their eggs, often found in cereal grains, nuts, and spices, can be eliminated. At the dosages used, the foods themselves are unaffected.[9]

Many fruits are presently marketed green, or at least picked and shipped unripe, because if they were fully tree-ripened, they would be subject to quick spoilage from rot. For this reason, many of the best varieties of apples are not even marketed and many other fruits, such as plums, peaches, papayas, pineapples, mangoes, and other tropical fruits, never attain their full flavor because of having to be picked green. Irradiation would change that, allowing fully ripened fruit to be marketed.

Strawberries are protected from mildew, and milk from souring or rotting, by radiation procedures. With all of these possible applications, and such obvious advantages in protecting food from spoilage, why aren't irradiated foods available in America's markets? The sad answer to that question lies in at least three areas.

First, although all the foods mentioned above have been approved for irradiation by the Food and Drug Administration, only a few market tests have been conducted (on mangoes in Florida and papayas in California). Ironically, the irradiated fruits have sold better than the non-irradiated produce—by ten to one—because of better appearance and superior flavor. Even so, by a federal law passed in 1958, radiation is arbitrarily defined as an "additive" to food. Although irradiation leaves no residue in food and does not and cannot make the food itself radioactive, the producer of irradiated food destined for the commercial market must go through clearances, testing, and licensing procedures so onerous and expensive that, so far, only government can afford to do it. New proposals for regulating irradiated foods are under consideration; they would accept the guidelines set out in 1980 by international health and food organizations and the United Nations Codex Alimentarius Commission and remove unnecessary barriers. This has already been done in several European countries.

Second, American food companies have expressed an interest only in irradiating spices, cocoa, and starch. For all other foods, as one executive put it, "large food companies have shown about as much interest in irradiation as they have in marketing acorns." Considering the enormous investment and commitment to current methods of food handling—such as chemical fumigants and refrigeration—this attitude is understandable. But with the banning of the most common fumigant, ethylene dibromide, and the problems that would arise with refrigeration should freon be banned, the future may bring about changes favorable to irradiation.

Third, there is opposition. The same opponents, including the Ralph Nader organizations that are against so many other products of technology, have instituted a campaign against irradiated food. These critics complain that not enough research on wholesomeness has been conducted, although studies have been carried out since 1943, when the U.S. Army Quartermaster Corps began research on the radiation preservation of food with the Food Science Department of the Massachusetts Institute of Technology. The opponents of irradiated food also focus on its use in Third World countries, where fully one quarter and sometimes up to 50 percent of the food is lost to spoilage and rot. The critics object to high technology (irradiators) being used in developing countries, even though 135 irradiators now operate in 42 countries around the world. Advocates claim that food irradiation will help solve some of the problems of Third World hunger, will replace expensive heat and refrigeration processes, and will reduce the incidence of foodborne disease. [10] Critics disagree—but fail to provide facts to support their position.

Given these factors—that 42 nations now approve the use of irradiated food; that 19 European nations, including the U.S.S.R., now process irradiated food; and that China plans to have a food irradiation plant in each major city[11] (five demonstration plants are already under construction)—it may be that the United States, which pioneered the process, could be the last nation to use it. So be it.

Most people believe that we don't need irradiated food. Yet, an estimated 10 to 15 million people suffer salmonella poisoning in the United States every year; several thousand die. Botulism is too common and trichina infestation of American pork is a disgrace. All told, there are between 24 to 80 million food-borne illnesses annually.

No one claims that food irradiation is appropriate for all foods in all situations. No one suggests that it will solve all of the world's hunger problems. No one says it will eliminate food poisoning. It is simply one more process for preserving food, one that has demonstrable advantages over refrigeration, freezing, canning, drying, salting, or smoking. Each of these procedures has its unique features and appropriate uses. So has irradiation, which is also helpful at the other end of the food chain: sewage.

We humans probably cause no greater insult to the natural environment than by our habit of depositing our sewage into lakes, streams, rivers, and oceans. Actually, sewage is a valuable source of organic material and nutrients, such as nitrogen and phosphorus. This has been well demonstrated in some Asian countries, where sewage has been used for centuries as a fertilizer. In recent years, after settling and removal of solids (primary treatment), sewage effluent has been sprayed in nutrient-poor forested areas with beneficial effect on tree growth. Similarly, the sludge left after de-wetting has proved its worth as a soil conditioner and fertilizer.

But public opposition to these uses is widespread, and most sewage is therefore "thrown away," usually under circumstances in which it overwhelms and degrades the environment. Recognizing the public's legitimate fears of the possible disease-causing organisms in human sewage, the U.S. Atomic Energy Commission developed a process to sterilize it using irradiation. The gamma-emitting isotope, Cesium-137, is removed from nuclear waste and packaged in an irradiator. On an endless belt running through the irradiator, bagged and de-watered sewage sludge is conveyed on pallets. For several years in the 1970s, a demonstration sewage sterilizing plant was operated for the city of Albuquerque, New Mexico. It was highly successful. Its product proved to be sterile, harmless, and valuable as a fertilizer, a soil conditioner, and even as an additive to cattle fodder. Surely, this is the preferred way to handle our growing sewage problems.

Radioisotopes have many other applications. Strontium-90 and Plutonium-238, which is formed from Neptunium-237 by neutron capture, are used for reliable, long-lived radioactive thermo-electric generators. These generators (RTGs) have been used to power more than a dozen space missions, including lunar experiments. Flight-grade Plutonium-238 has been in Martian landers, was used in inter-planetary spacecraft to explore Jupiter, Saturn, Neptune, and Uranus, and in the remarkable Explorer journey to the edge of our planetary system and beyond. Doesn't anybody ever wonder how those remark-able photographs are sent back to earth? Power from Plutonium-238, of course. Isotopic power sources (RTGs)[12] have performed for more than ten million mission hours without failure in space, marine, and terrestrial environments, at weather stations, and at remote ocean locations. They are inherently rugged, reliable, independent, and enduring. They supply useful electric power in the multiwatt range in remote and hostile environments for 15 to 20 years without refueling or maintenance. They function totally unattended, are safe, and the fuel comes from isotopes separated out of nuclear waste.

Electronic lights using beta-emitting isotopes, such as Krypton-85, a waste product of commercial power plants, or tritium, interacting with a phosphor, have been developed for both military and civilian applications. Krypton or tritium lights, glowing with a yellow-green radioluminescence, are rugged, can be air-dropped, and have been tested for use on remote airfields in Alaska. They have now been installed on several airfields in Alaskan villages.[13] When used in locations away from the glow of city lights, they are visible up to seven miles. They operate over a temperature range from 62 degrees Centi-grade below zero to 54 degrees Centigrade above and endure for some 10 to 20 years. Because they cannot spark and therefore cause fires, they have obvious applications in oil refineries and chemical plants.

Americium-243, used in building and household smoke detectors, has protected untold thousands of people from death or injury in fires. Other radioisotopes have made possible a whole new field of non-destructive testing in industry, from checking the reliability of welds and joints to detecting cracks, measuring the thickness of paper, and hundreds of other applications.[14] Neutron radiography is ideal for non-destructive examination of such objects as electronic components and carbon fiber composites of airplane wings.

Technetium-99, in addition to its value in nuclear medicine, can replace platinum as a catalyst in refining hydrocarbon fuels. Carbon-14 is used to establish the date or age of artifacts—and so the applications grow.

In basic science, isotopes and nuclear science in general have aided physicists to gain deeper insight into the structure of matter and the nature of the universe. Radioisotopes have helped chemists to unravel the complexities of chemical reactions and to understand the architecture of molecules. The use of radioisotopes is indispensable to biologists in their quest to understand the intricacies of cellular function and gene modification. The explosion of knowledge in the basic sciences over the last 30 years is to a considerable degree a consequence of understanding and applying nuclear science.

Isotopes are here to stay.

Chapter 10

POWER FROM THE ATOM, THE SUN, AND THE WIND

O F ALL THE CIVILIAN applications of nuclear science, none has generated more opposition than the production of electricity.[1] It is worth noting, however, that in the early years of nuclear power (from the mid-1960s to the early 1970s) it was enthusiastically supported by the Audubon Society, the Sierra Club, and the public in general. The turnaround came after there developed a widespread feeling that nuclear power had failed to live up to its early promise and that it might have encountered unanticipated problems. This belief was actively promoted at a 1973 gathering called "Critical Mass," sponsored by Ralph Nader. Since then, nearly all environmental groups have joined the anti-nuclear camp and much of the general public has become suspicious of nuclear power.

Yet, by any measure except in public relations, nuclear power is an unparalleled success. Nuclear generation of electricity is safe. In the more than a quarter century of commercial operation in the United States and the Western World, there have been no fatalities, no significant releases of radioactivity to the environment, and no one has been exposed to radiation in excess of the very conservative limits that have always characterized the nuclear industry.[2]

One hundred and twelve nuclear power plants are now operating in the United States, and they have amassed more than 1,200 reactor years of experience. They produce 20 percent of our nation's electricity. In 1988, domestic nuclear power plants turned out 450 billion kilowatt hours; that is more than the entire electrical output of the United States in the early 1950s.[3]

Nuclear power has saved $100 billion in foreign oil payments since 1973. The electricity is produced without releasing carbon dioxide, sulfur oxides, nitrogen oxides, smoke, particulate matter, organic compounds, or carcinogens to the atmosphere. Additionally, the amount of solid waste (ash) resulting from nuclear power is far less than the amounts produced by burning coal and is without such residues as arsenic, lead, cadmium, and mercury that remain toxic forever. No nuclear plant turns out electricity at so high a cost as one burning oil, and all are competitive with coal-burning facilities. When lifetime costs are calculated over a 30-year cycle and compared, for example, with oil-burning facilities, all nuclear plants average 4.7 cents per kilowatt hour, whereas at the lowest oil prices even the best oil burners average nearly double that: 8.2 cents per kilowatt hour. If one selects only recent, more costly nuclear plants, those going on-line in 1984–87, they average 7.6 cents per kilowatt hour, still less than the lowest cost oil burners and still competitive with electricity generated by burning coal. Most of the industrial world and several developing nations are committed to nuclear power and to the light water reactor (LWR), the basic reactor design that was engineered and commercialized in the United States.[4] As of May 1989, France generated 69.9 percent of its electricity through nuclear power. In Belgium the rate is 65.5 percent, in Hungary 48.9 percent, Sweden 46.9 percent, South Korea 46.9 percent, Taiwan 41 percent, Switzerland 37.4 percent, Spain 36.1 percent, Finland 36.2 percent, Bulgaria 35.6 percent, West Germany 34 percent, Japan 28.3 percent, Czechoslovakia 26.7 percent, the United States 20 percent, the United Kingdom 19.3 percent, Canada 16 percent, the U.S.S.R. 12.6 percent, and Argentina 1.2 percent.

The percentage of the total amount of electricity generated by nuclear power tells only part of the story; it is also instructive to know how many nuclear plants are operating. Here, America leads the list with its 112. Second is the Soviet Union with 60 operating, 33 in construction, and 44 more planned. France is next with 53 operating and nine more in various phases of construction. Japan has 33 operating and is constructing 17 more. East Germany has 12 operating reactors and South Korea has six completed and six in construction. All told, worldwide, 41 nations are operating a total of 407 nuclear power plants. Every sixth kilowatt hour of electricity produced in the world comes from nuclear generation.

The electricity delivered from the world's nuclear plants *since* April 26, 1986—the date of the Chernobyl plant accident in the U.S.S.R., when some predicted the end of nuclear power—exceeds 3,000 billion kilowatt hours. Had this amount of electricity been generated by burning fossil fuel, it would have required 500 million tons of oil or one billion tons of coal. Incidentally, if coal had been used, an additional three billion tons of carbon dioxide, 20 million tons of sulfur dioxide, and five million tons of nitrous oxide would have been discharged into the atmosphere.

Given this positive record of clean, safe, economic operation, why is there controversy regarding nuclear power plants?[5] The objections appear to be four in number: fear that the power plants will release radioactivity, fear of the consequences of a major accident, worry about the disposal of nuclear waste, and belief that there are better, alternative ways to produce electricity. Each of these objections deserves serious attention.

First, with respect to the release of radioactivity, nuclear power plants are very strictly regulated by the Nuclear Regulatory Commission (NRC) and the ambient radioactivity is monitored by both state agencies and by the Environmental Protection Agency. Permissible radiation from a nuclear power plant may not exceed five millirems per year; actually most plants do far better and emit only between one and three millirems per year. To put this amount into perspective, recall that the average background radiation exposure for every person in America is 350 mrem/year, one chest X-ray delivers about 50 mrems, and passengers on a coast-to-coast jet flight receive about five mrem, the same as smoking a single cigarette.

Of course, there have been times when nuclear plants released measurable amounts of radioactivity to the environment, but these were only a very small fraction of the background radiation. Even in the fearsome accident at Three Mile Island, the worst ever suffered in the United States, the average exposure to the population living nearby was 1.2 mrem, and the maximum amount right at the plant itself was well below 100 mrem. People who live in highly insulated, energy-conserving homes are exposed to far more radioactivity (from radon) than those who live near nuclear facilities. They also receive more radiation than those who actually work in nuclear power plants. The entire nuclear industry, including all nuclear power plants, contributes less than one percent of all the radiation in the environment. No ill effect has ever been experienced from these minute amounts of radio-activity.

Second, the possibility of a major accident and the consequences of that occurrence at a nuclear power plant have been exhaustively studied. The worst possible accident would be a meltdown of the intensely radioactive fuel, with release of radioactivity to the environment. Such an accident could happen in a light water reactor if the flow of coolant water were to be interrupted. For that reason, there are many backup and redundant safety systems to guard against that possibility and there is a totally independent supply of cooling water (ECCS, or Emergency Core Cooling System). Even so, an accident that damaged the fuel did happen at Three Mile Island, and it demon-strated the importance of the containment safety feature. Radioactivity did escape from the reactor itself, but it was held within the containment building, much of it "plating out" on the inner walls. Indeed, it can be said with confidence that the most important result of the Three Mile Island accident was that it proved the engineered safety systems worked even better than expected. No living creature was harmed by the radioactivity and no environmental damage occurred. The only damage was restricted to the reactor and to the plant itself. It was costly, but as with so many other technologies, the accident led to important improvements in both plant design and operation.

Could another accident like it occur at another nuclear power plant? Yes, but there is every confidence that any radioactivity released would be safely contained within the building. Theoretically, however, the safety systems might fail, and a real meltdown accident might occur. Risk analysis studies estimate that a meltdown could happen once in every 20,000 years of reactor operation. We now have had more than 1,000 reactor years in the commercial arena and 3,000 reactor years in naval ship propulsion. The risk analysis studies estimate that one in every 5,000 meltdowns would release radioactivity that might result in as many as 1,000 deaths. Again, to put that calculated risk into perspective, there are about 10,000 deaths every year from using coal to generate electricity, so for nuclear power to be as dangerous as coal-burning, we would have to have a great many meltdown accidents per year. Since we have not had any and there have been no fatalities at all, clearly nuclear power is safer than using coal.

Of course, it is possible to imagine an accident in which absolutely everything goes wrong and no one takes corrective action. Such a "scenario" has also been analyzed. It would result in about 50,000 deaths. It has a probability of occurring once in a billion years of reactor operation. As Dr. Bernard Cohen, a University of Pittsburgh physicist who is one of the nation's foremost risk analysis experts, says, "No one in his right mind worries about such improbable events."[6]

Third, the problems with nuclear waste are legion, but they are not technical. They are emotional and political. They are examined in the next chapter.

Fourth, what about alternatives to nuclear power?[7] Can't we use something else? Of all the ways of producing energy, none has greater appeal than solar power. After all, there's the sun sending all that heat and light and radiation to the earth for free—so why not harness it? And it makes good sense. Solar heat is used in many places (including Florida and the Southwestern United States) to heat water for domestic use, to heat swimming pools, and even to heat homes or augment the heating of buildings. Taking advantage of the warmth of natural sunlight is one of the enlightened ways to conserve energy.

But solar water heaters also require maintenance, and even with large tax subsidies it turns out that conventional appliances like gas-fueled water heaters, for example, are much cheaper to install and maintain, run for pennies a day, and operate dependably, even when the sun isn't shining. Ways to store solar heat are inefficient and expensive. As a result, solar water-heating has never caught on or penetrated the market on its own merits.

It is also possible to produce electricity by harnessing sunlight if— and here's the big "if"—all you need is a few watts, not kilowatts or megawatts, of electricity and if you are willing to pay exorbitant prices for it. The space program is one example of an appropriate use of solar energy. Solar cells produce electricity in space for several orbiting satellites—although not for deep space probes that range far from the sun or for spacecraft like the shuttle that require large amounts of power. Solar cells have also found an application for powering sensors, repeaters, beacons, and recording devices in remote and inaccessible places. But to produce large amounts of electricity—such as are needed to run a home with modern appliances (vacuum cleaners, dishwashers, irons, washing machines, dryers, stoves, toasters, coffee makers, food processors, electric blankets, modern lighting, and so on) or to run a city or a business or an industrial operation—solar generated electricity is not a practical alternative.[8]

Why not? Because, to begin with, sunlight is diffuse. To use it as a source of electricity, solar radiation must first be collected and concentrated. Two analogies help illustrate the point.

First, suppose you wish to boil a pot of water and all you have is a bunch of matches. No matter how many matches are used, the water cannot be heated to boiling by holding them, one by one, under the pot. The heat thus applied is too diffuse. Even burning all the matches at once will not do the job. There is simply not enough heat concentrated for a long enough time. To achieve the required temperature, concentrated energy must be used, such as that produced by igniting burning material, wood, coal, charcoal, gas, or oil.

The other analogy is my all-time favorite, for it dramatically illustrates the importance of concentrated energy. It goes like this:

In biology, there is a term, "biomass," which refers to the total amount of living material in any body or collection of living things. Thus, you can compare the biomass equivalents of different species; for example, there is the same biomass in the body of one elephant as there is in 100 million fleas. Now, if you need to pull a very heavy load, would you rather harness one elephant or 100 million fleas? Provided, of course, that someone builds flea harnesses at a price you can afford to pay, and provided, of course, that you can make all those fleas hop at the same time and in the same direction!

And that explains the trouble with solar power. It is diffuse and, like the fleas, it is difficult and expensive to organize and concentrate.

At best—that is, at noon on a sunny day—sunlight strikes the earth with an energy of about one kilowatt per square meter. There is no way to make the sun shine hotter or to collect more energy from sunlight, except to capture the one kilowatt per square meter from a very large area.

Solar collectors, therefore, are necessary. They can be built using mirrors or lenses, but these must be installed with small motors so they can tilt and rotate and be kept in position with relation to the sun as the earth turns on its axis. They must also be programmed to follow the sun in its seasonal cycle. Such a solar plant has been built, largely with taxpayers' dollars, of course, by Southern California Edison at Barstow, California.[9] Called Solar One, it covers 75 acres with one million square feet of mirrors, 11,818 mirrors in all, each computer-driven to reflect sunlight onto a water tower 300 feet tall. With some storage devices, Solar One can generate ten megawatts at a cost of $14,000 per installed kilowatt. This is about five times more costly than the most expensive nuclear plant.

On cloudless days, Solar One can generate at full power for eight hours a day in the summer, four hours a day in the winter. Assuming nothing goes wrong and the mirrors remain clean, that means Solar One has an availability of somewhere between 17 percent and 33 percent; nuclear power plants and conventionally fueled energy plants have an availability of about 65 to 70 percent. In other words, Solar One produces about one percent of the amount of electricity of a nuclear or coal-fired plant on five times the space and is available only a quarter of the day. And the total cost? About eight times more expensive. Even without the question of availability, solar power is no bargain. Nor is the expense likely to come down, given the prodigious amount of materials needed to build a large electricity-producing solar plant—about a thousand times more material than for a similar-sized coal or nuclear plant—plus the cost of operation and maintenance (who cleans all those mirrors?).

To construct a 1,000 megawatt solar plant, the following amounts of material are needed: 35,000 tons of aluminum, two million tons of concrete (500 times more than for a nuclear plant), 7,500 tons of copper, 600,000 tons of steel, 75,000 tons of glass, and 1,500 tons of chromium and titanium.

Solar One was seriously damaged by an explosion and fire on August 31, 1986. The 240,000 gallons of mineral oil—used because of the EPA regulations against PCBs—caught fire and burned; the temperature reached 600 degrees Fahrenheit. [10]

Although Solar One operated by collecting and focusing the sun's heat, direct conversion of solar radiation into electricity can also be accomplished by using solar cells: photovoltaics. Whichever method is adopted, solar heat or photovoltaics, a large amount of land is needed, about 50 square miles for a 1,000 megawatt plant. Compare this to the 75 to 150 acres for a 1,000 megawatt nuclear or coal plant. Suppose the eight million people of New York City were to be served by photovoltaic solar power. [11] To supply 7,000 megawatts of electricity, New York City would need at least 350 square miles of solar cells, an area larger than the city itself.

Although the cost for photovoltaic cells has come down from $10 per peak watt in the early 1980s to $5 per peak watt today, that is still high. The cost of a solar-powered home unit offered by Photocomm, Inc., that provides four kilowatts is $7,377. A five kilowatt gasoline-powered generator is sold by Honda for $650 and has the advantage of running *all* the time.

In 1979, the Southern Railway installed solar cells on the roof of a caboose to power the train's tail lights. But it was found that the added weight required more energy to pull the caboose than the solar cells could generate, even in bright sunlight. [12]

In summary, there are appropriate applications for solar energy, but that does not include producing large amounts of electricity. Moreover, photovoltaic cells are truly high-tech, and considerable energy is required for their manufacture; their construction also requires toxic materials from cadmium to hydrofluoric acid. This, together with the large maintenance problem involved in keeping the collectors, mirrors, lenses, and solar cells free from dust, greasy films, and snow, combines to make solar power one of the least safe ways to generate electricity. [13] Since the number two cause of accidental deaths in the United States is falls (20,000 deaths per year; auto accidents are number one at 50,000) and cleaning the solar collecting surfaces requires climbing onto roofs or supporting structures, solar energy is considered physically dangerous. Risk analysis studies rate solar plants more dangerous than nuclear or fossil fuel plants. [14]

Like solar power, the energy generated by windmills ultimately comes from the sun, since that is what sets the atmosphere in motion. Also like solar power, windmills have legitimate and important applications in *some* places and for *some* purposes. They have been used for many years to pump water, and when placed in persistently windy areas—such as the North Sea coast of the Netherlands or much of the American Midwest—they work very well for this purpose. But producing electricity introduces significant problems.

In remote and windy areas, where connections to a transmission line are unlikely, windmills can produce modest amounts of electricity, given favorable winds that blow steadily at about 15 miles per hour. [15] For the last two decades, substantial efforts have been expended to develop windmill technology to the point where multi-kilowatt to megawatt amounts of electricity can be demonstrated. Most of these efforts have failed and been abandoned. Some representative windmill projects are the following:

1. A two megawatt windmill with 100-foot blades built with $30 million ($15,000 per installed kilowatt) of taxpayers' money by Southern California Edison. It rarely worked and was auctioned for salvage in 1983 for $51,000. [16]

2. In Alameda County, California, at Altamont Pass in the hills between Oakland and Stockton, up to 7,000 windmills have been installed. The noise, when they operate, is so great that the operators have had to establish a fund to buy out nearby homeowners who sue. Said one: "You can hear that continuous whipping, whistling roar only

for so long before you go raving mad." Many of the 7,000 windmills are not operating. Maintenance problems have proved to be severe. Wind never blows steadily or evenly. It pulses, and that contributes to the unpleasant sound and the stresses on the vanes. [17] Also, significant numbers of birds, including eagles, are killed by flying into the whirling blades.

3. Experimental windmill "farms" in North Carolina and Vermont have been closed down because of noise complaints from neighbors, and in the Goodnoe Hills of the Columbia Gorge in Washington State an ambitious windmill project failed because of too many breakdowns.

Despite discouraging experience, private industry has been quite successful in developing small (17 to 600 kilowatt) machines that are dependable and economic. There are about 17,000 such turbines in California. U.S. Windpower operates 3,400 windmills of 100 kilowatts each in the Altamont Pass.

If windmills prove to work as their designers intend and without expensive maintenance, how many would it take to make a major contribution to this nation's electricity supply? According to a study done at Lockheed, wind power could supply 19 percent of America's power with 63,000 windmills having towers over 300 feet high, blades 100 feet across, and a steady wind. No one has suggested where these machines might be installed.

Since recent experience demonstrates that smaller windmills are more dependable and efficient, the number required to make a 19 percent contribution to the United States electricity supply is probably much larger than the 63,000 identified in the Lockheed study. [18]

I cannot leave the subject of wind power without recounting the story of the world's first and only (though temporary) nuclear-powered windmill. It came about, inadvertently I'm sure, in 1980, when a group of students at the University of Wisconsin planned a rock-music concert, where the electricity needed for lighting, sound amplification, and other needs was to be supplied by solar power. But when the students found they would need at least two acres of solar collectors, they settled for three windmills instead. Came the day of the concert— and no wind. But the students had taken this problem into account and switched to their backup system, which was a hookup to the city of Madison's electrical supply. The windmills turned nicely, although one of them went backward. Since 32 percent of Madison's power comes from nuclear plants, it could be said that one of the three windmills used by the students *was nuclear-powered*! Irony of ironies. [19]

Wood waste, biomass, geothermal, wind, photovoltaic, and solar thermal power presently supply less than one percent of the nation's electricity. This may increase and it may even double or triple, but for the foreseeable future, it will not make much of a difference.

We are left, then, with the sober fact that 99 percent of the electricity in the United States is produced from only three sources, and one of these, hydropower at four to six percent of the total, is not likely to expand. That leaves us with nuclear power at 20 percent and fossil fuel-burning for the remaining 75 percent. Of the latter, coal accounts for about 60 percent and oil and natural gas for about 15 percent. These proportions will not change easily or very soon.

Since nuclear and coal are the only fuels available to produce the large quantities of electricity needed in today's world, it is both instructive and important to compare the relative environmental consequences of their use. [20]

First, comparing the effluents from a 1,000 megawatt electric (MWe) coal plant with a nuclear plant of similar size reveals that the coal plant produces carbon dioxide at a rate of 500 pounds per second or seven million tons per year; the nuclear plant produces none. The coal plant produces sulfur oxides at a rate of one ton every five minutes, 120,000 tons per year; the nuclear plant produces none. The coal plant produces nitrogen oxides equivalent to 200,000 automobiles, 20,000 tons per year; the nuclear plant produces none. The coal plant produces quantities of smoke whose large particles are generally filtered out, but the small, dangerous ones remain and are spread widely; the nuclear plant produces none. The coal plant produces more than 40 different organic compounds that are released without control to the atmosphere; the nuclear plant produces none. Finally, since all coal contains some uranium, radium, and thorium, coal plants release unmonitored amounts of radioactivity; the only radioactive element released to the atmosphere by nuclear power plants is Krypton-85, a harmless, noble gas, which is released in minute quantities under strict control.

Turning to solid waste, it is produced in a coal-burning plant at a rate of 1,000 pounds per minute, or 750,000 tons per year; the annual amount of spent fuel from a nuclear plant is about 50 tons. The hazardous ingredients in coal ash include arsenic, mercury, cadmium, and lead, all of which maintain the same degree of toxicity forever. This material is discharged to the environment *without controls*. The nuclear plants' spent fuel continuously loses radioactivity, eventually decaying to background levels. Disposal of nuclear waste is strictly controlled. The annual amount of fuel required for a 1,000 megawatt coal-burning plant amounts to 38,000 rail cars of coal, three million tons per year; for a nuclear plant of similar size, six truckloads, or about 50 tons of fuel per year (and that includes the heavy metal-carrying casks), are all that are used.

The lack of environmental effect in using nuclear power relates to the fact that the process does not involve chemical combustion and operates on the principle of containing wastes, not dispersing them.

The heat that is produced and released—the thermal discharge—is about the same from a coal-burning unit as from a nuclear one, and it can readily be turned to useful purposes; for example, heating greenhouses. In Sweden, nuclear-produced steam has been used to heat homes and buildings. And in Switzerland, a new type of passive reactor, called Geyser,[21] has been designed for the purpose of space heating. The ten megawatt Canadian reactor called Slowpoke has been proposed for heating the entire campus of the University of Saskatchewan.[22] Some nuclear plants discharge their waste heat directly into water, where the slightly elevated temperatures prove beneficial to fish. At the Turkey Point plant in Florida, the warmed water is used as a breeding area for alligators.

Since many of the wastes from coal-burning plants are airborne, their ultimate disposal takes place on land, in water, and, of course, in people's lungs. Comparative risk studies put the health effects of coal burning at about 50,000 fatalities annually. From nuclear power there are none.

Given the clear advantage and successful operation of nuclear power, why is the nuclear power plant situation in the United States always portrayed as so dismal?[23] The public is constantly reminded that there have been no new plant orders in a decade—even though there have been no new orders for coal plants, oil-fired plants, or big dams either. Only gas turbines, very expensive but uncomplicated to build, have made a real addition to generating capacity.[24] Cogeneration has held out great promises, but it has been unreliable and its promises unrealized.

The public is also constantly reminded of the half-dozen or so troubled nuclear plants—but never informed about the 100 or more that are operating properly and efficiently. Nor is the public informed about the attention paid to safety, both in construction and in operation. Since the early 1970s, because of concerns about safety, the amount of steel required to build a 1,000 megawatt nuclear power plant has increased by 41 percent, the amount of concrete by 27 percent, the footage of pipe by 50 percent, the amount of electrical cable by 36 percent, and the number of man hours of labor by 50 percent. All these improvements have increased construction costs, and still nuclear plants are cost-competitive.[25]

The nuclear power industry has developed a program to assure that information about problems and performance is quickly exchanged. Nuclear utilities now all belong to the Institute for Nuclear Power Operations (INPO), which is dedicated to assuring safe, dependable, efficient operations. The record of improvement in the last decade is evidence of the effectiveness of INPO, as is the fact that it has served as a model for the recently formed World Association of Nuclear Operators (WANO). Moreover, the work force now is better trained, and many fundamental phenomena, such as stress corrosion cracking, are far better understood. Risk analysis is consistently practiced and the results are used to identify and correct potential problems.

Without doubt, today's nuclear power reactors are safe, but the questions persist: Are they safe enough? How safe is safe enough? How is safety judged? And by whom? If engineered safety—that is, multiple, redundant backup systems or "defense in depth"—is safe, how much enhancement is needed? How much is wanted? Or warranted?

At what point should the cost of yet another marginal increment in safety be considered?[26]

It is interesting to note that in our society, $200,000 is spent annually on safety improvements to save a single life in an automobile accident—where 50,000 deaths occur each year. But in the nuclear industry $2 billion is spent yearly to save one life, even though there have been no fatalities.[27] Is there such a thing as "inherently safe" or an "inherently safe system"? These questions have been given considerable attention in the nuclear industry.

In this regard, the Congressional Report on the Department of Defense budget for 1989 quotes a recent court action. The question before the court was whether the Nuclear Regulatory Commission (NRC) had required the needed margin of safety for nuclear power plants. The report states:

> The Court of Appeals (Washington, D.C.) held that under the adequate protection standard, "the NRC need ensure only an acceptable or adequate level of protection to public health and safety; the NRC need not demand that nuclear power plants present *no* risk of harm. The level of adequate protection need not, and almost certainly will not, be the level of zero risk. This court has long held that the adequate protection standard permits the acceptance of some level of risk."

While the debate continues about how safe light water reactors are—and their record is impressive—research continues to improve them still further. In addition, other reactor types have been developed whose safe operation depend more upon fundamental physical principles, and less upon engineered safety systems and well trained operators. Nuclear reactors other than the current light water or heavy water types are often called "advanced reactors," even though the basic concepts may have been around for a long time.[28]

Historically, the light water reactor became the standard for generating electricity in the United States because the technology was already developed and proved in the propulsion reactor for submarines. It was not difficult, from an engineering standpoint, to convert the reactor that had been designed to provide energy to the drive shaft of a ship and apply that same energy to turbines for generating electricity.

While performing admirably, the light water reactor has some features that render it a complex and unforgiving technology. To begin with, it has a high power density. This comes from its origin in the naval propulsion reactor, where the power density is important, but it is not required to generate electricity. Second, the light water technology requires an active response for all possible malfunctions; this means that a multitude of engineered safety systems are needed, from automatic shutoff valves, to an extra supply of cooling water, to emergency backup diesel power to operate pumps and circulate the coolant. It is a great credit to the ingenuity and competence of nuclear engineers that the defense-in-depth systems operate so well. Third, light water reactors require constant attention and monitoring by operators trained to react within a few minutes in the case of a malfunction.

Research on light water reactors now under way is directed toward more passive safety, reducing the number of valves, pumps, tanks, etc., and making greater use of gravity, convection, natural circulation, and stored energy to remove decay heat. Both types of light water reactors in the United States—the pressurized water reactor developed by Westinghouse and General Electric's boiling water reactor—have advanced designs that incorporate these safety features based on physical principles. [29]

Another design that incorporates automatic safety features has been developed in Sweden. Called Process Inherent Ultimate Safety (PIUS), [30] the reactor core is permanently connected to a large pool of borated water with a thermohydraulic arrangement, so that any incident that could otherwise lead to inadequate cooling is immediately terminated by flooding. The amount of water containing boron, which impedes the fission process, is sufficient to keep the reactor fuel cool for a minimum of one week—plenty of time to take other corrective actions.

Another type of reactor, the Modular High Temperature Gas-cooled Reactor (MHTGR), [31] has had a long developmental history. An early version, Peach Bottom 1 (40 megawatts), was successfully operated by the Philadelphia Electric Company from 1967 to 1984, achieving a remarkable 88 percent availability. A much larger plant, Fort St. Vrain, at 330 megawatts, has been built and operated by the Colorado Public Service. It experienced continuing problems with circulating pumps and leaking lubrication, but this was in the balance of the plant and was not related to the reactor itself, which demonstrated excellent fuel performance.

The basic features of the MHTGR consist of unique fuel design with the enriched uranium contained within ceramic microspheres, graphite moderator, and inert helium coolant.

The ceramic-coated fuel particles retain their structural integrity and do not release radionuclides, even at extreme temperatures up to 2,000 degrees Centigrade. Operating temperatures are 538 degrees Centigrade for steam and 687 degrees for the helium coolant as it leaves the core. Each reactor module is housed in a vertical concrete cylinder that is fully recessed underground. The system is designed so that decay heat can be rejected to the earth, again without loss of integrity or release of radionuclides. Reserve shutdown capability is provided by boron pellets inserted into separate channels next to the fuel rods. A single control room can handle up to four reactor modules.

Because of the relatively small size (538 megawatts), modular construction, and the design simplicity which applies also to maintenance and operation, the MHTGR is well suited to the needs of smaller utilities and to the emerging demands for electricity in developing countries. Another advantage of the MHTGR is that, besides electricity, it can produce the high temperature steam useful for many industrial applications. Finally, the fuel, enclosed within ceramic microspheres, is completely contained, therefore easing the problem of "spent fuel."

One of the most unusual and promising of all the advanced reactor concepts is the Integral Fast Reactor (IFR)[32] developed at the Argonne National Laboratory in Chicago. Its fuel is metal, an alloy of uranium, plutonium, and zirconium, and it utilizes liquid metal (sodium) cooling. The high thermal conductivity of the metallic fuel permits low fuel operating temperatures, and the enormous thermal inertia of liquid sodium allows a pool-type configuration where no circulation of coolant is required. Operations can be conducted at normal atmospheric pressure, making a thick-walled pressure vessel unnecessary. The boiling temperature of sodium is above 900 degrees Centigrade; the coolant operating temperatures are much lower, ranging from 350 degrees at the inlet to 510 at the outlet. Thus, there is an ample margin for safe operations. Moreover, the metallic fuel can be fabricated on site by compact metallurgical processing and injection casting in a single step, and it can be reprocessed by electrochemical refining. These features allow the fuel cycle to be closed, with all the steps—fuel fabrication, burnup in the reactor, and fuel reprocessing—conducted at the same locale, thus minimizing the transportation of radioactive materials. And the use of electro-refining techniques conducted at temperatures around 500 degrees means that the amount of waste involved in reprocessing is drastically reduced. No liquid waste is produced. This unique, contained fuel cycle gives rise to the reactor's name designation—integral.

In the IFR design, there is no moderator and the neutrons released are therefore not slowed; hence the designation, "fast" reactor. Besides the designed safety of the IFR, whose automatic shutdown characteristics have been demonstrated under every conceivable accident situation, this reactor has another possible application beyond the generation of electricity. The abundance of fast neutrons it produces can be used for the transmutation of certain radionuclides. Both in the military programs and in the current light water reactors of the civilian economy, large quantities of high level wastes have accumulated. Those designated as "transuranic" (TRU) wastes (that is, those containing radionuclides heavier than uranium) can be degraded to a stable or nonradioactive state if exposed to fast neutrons. The IFR is capable of doing this and can thereby make a major contribution toward solving nuclear waste problems.

This brief discussion of advanced reactors would not be complete without mention of two other recent developments. First there is the Geyser,[33] a small, thermohydraulically controlled reactor developed in Switzerland for the purpose of heating water which is then circulated to provide home and building heat. This little reactor has low power density, high designed-in safety, is self-regulating according to hydraulic principles, and operates in the almost complete absence of human attendance. An operator need only check the gauges every few days. Conventional fuel elements of the light water reactor type with 8 to 20 percent enrichment are used. They give a power range of 10 to 50 megawatts (thermal, since no electricity is generated) and have a core life of 15 years, after which the core itself is simply replaced. The entire reactor and coolant assembly is recessed in a buried concrete pit 35 to 50 meters deep. The production of neutrons is controlled by borated water in a self-adjusting thermohydraulic process, and the water that actually circulates for district heating is contained in a closed heat-transfer system. A full-scale, non-nuclear model thirty-two meters high has successfully demonstrated the Geyser system and proved that it is, indeed, self-operating and "walk away" safe.

The second new design, using existing and proven technology in a unique manner, is called the Compact Nuclear Power Source (CNPS).[34] It is a small reactor that has been designed to provide the small amounts of electricity (15 to 40 kilowatts) needed to operate the radars installed along what used to be called the Dew Line—the North Warning System.

The reactor, a six-foot-high by six-foot-wide prototype weighing six tons, has been built at the Los Alamos National Laboratory in New Mexico. It is designed to be factory-built, fueled, and sealed, then transported to the site by ship, train, truck, helicopter, or plane, and lowered into the ground. After placement of a concrete cap, the only thing emerging from underground is an electrical outlet. The reactor is self-operating, requires no attendance, will produce electricity for 20 years, and is "walk away" safe.

The underground part consists of a concrete vault-like body containing the reactor core, which utilizes the well proven HTGR microsphere fuel embedded in graphite. The graphite block also contains a number of heat pipes, capped by thermoelectric modules. These thermoelectric units, capable of converting heat to electricity, have been used extensively in space and in other hostile or difficult environments. They have a remarkable record of success with few failures in unattended operation. Cooling is provided by natural air circulation and the operating temperature is about 630 degrees Centigrade.

A variation on this design to provide more power—up to 100 kilowatts—involves the addition of an Organic Rankine Cycle utilizing toluene. Such units have demonstrated high reliability to operate pumps on the Alaska pipeline. Their use would require some maintenance, perhaps as often as once a year.

Despite the obvious advantages of this small reactor and despite its applicability (with the Rankine Cycle) to provide reliable, safely produced electricity to remote villages, only the prototype has been built, and it has not been used. The problem—like many problems in the nuclear field—is not in our scientific or technological capabilities but in politics and bureaucratic infighting. This promising small reactor was sacrificed by the failure to conclude a simple memorandum of understanding with Canada. It is not given to the average citizen—or to an engineer or scientist—to understand the arcane ways of bureaucrats. Such is the fate of technology in America today.

Chapter 11

NUCLEAR WASTE

No OTHER ASPECT of nuclear science has so dominated and influenced the public's negative view of nuclear power as has nuclear waste.[1] And this is ironic, because in truth there is no real technical problem either in handling nuclear waste or in treating it. But the public *thinks* that the "problem of nuclear waste" has not been "solved." Has the problem of waste from burning coal been "solved" by allowing the effluents to pollute the air and the ashes to be dispersed without control? The erroneous view is regularly put forward by nuclear critics and just as regularly publicized until it has become part of the folklore surrounding the nuclear enterprise.

Some of the widespread apprehension about nuclear waste relates to governmental indecision and temporizing, because now, more than 45 years after radioactive waste began to accumulate, the debate continues about what best to do with it. What is widely interpreted as the inability to find a solution is actually a political inability to implement any solution.[2]

Another source of apprehension is that much of the waste originated in the nation's military program. In the context of producing nuclear weapons, waste management was for a long time given low priority. From 1947 to 1953, urgency resided elsewhere. Those were the years that spanned the origin of the Atomic Energy Commission (AEC) and its assumption under civilian control of total responsibility for all nuclear activities.

In 1947, the AEC had little time for thoughts of the peaceful atom or radioactive waste. Soviet Russia, which had not yet learned how to build atomic weapons, rejected the American-United Nations control plan and was busy trying to build atomic bombs of its own. The AEC had just reported to President Truman that America's supposed shield of atomic bombs simply did not exist and that we had no reservoir of atomic weapons. Under those circumstances, the overwhelming attention of the AEC was on stockpiling weapons.

The AEC was preoccupied with stepping up plutonium production for the fabrication of warheads. Disposal of spent fuel was considered a secondary matter, and the question of producing electricity from such reactors still lay far into the future. The sense of urgency was over-whelming, as David E. Lilienthal, the first chairman of the AEC, indicated in his memoirs:[3]

In the late afternoon of April 3, 1947, I was in the oval room of the White House. As head of the newly created civilian Atomic Energy Commission, I had come to report to President Truman on the atomic energy establishment we had just taken over from the Army's wartime Manhattan District.

At this time, it was assumed by everyone, the President included, that America had a supply of atomic bombs. In fact, Winston Churchill was declaiming that it was our atomic stockpile that restrained the Soviet Union from moving in on the otherwise defenseless people of Europe. What we of the new A.E.C. had just discovered in taking inventory of nuclear materials and devices inherited from the Army was that this defense did not exist. There was no stockpile. There was not a single operable atomic bomb in the vault at Los Alamos, nor could there be one for many months to come.

This news was top secret, the biggest secret of that time; so secret that I did not commit it to paper, even as a part of the A.E.C.'s secret archive. As I gave President Truman this shocking information, the impact of the news was evident in his expression. . . . He turned to me, a grim, gray look on his face, the lines from his nose to his mouth visibly deepened.

At the end of the sobering meeting, we shook hands as usual and made
our good-byes.

I noted in my journal entry that the President was rather subdued and
thoughtful-looking. His customary joke on parting was missing, and
then in that abrupt jerky way of talking, he said:

"Come in to see me any time, just any time. I'll always be glad to see
you. You have the most important thing there is. You must make a
blessing of it or (with a half-grin as he pointed to a large globe in the
corner of his office) we'll blow that all to smithereens."

President Truman's injunction to make a blessing of the atom rang in
my ears from that day on. In that homely phrase, he expressed the hope
and purpose of all Americans, scientists and average citizens alike. This
became our job, our mission, to find a way to convert the virtually
unlimited power of nuclear fission into electric energy for the benefit of
all mankind.

But it would be some time before the peaceful uses of atomic energy
would emerge, and the new commission set up its priorities as follows:
first, to increase the supply of uranium ore; second, to increase the
supply of enriched uranium; third, to increase the production of
plutonium; and fourth, to increase the number of weapons.[4]

In 1949, the Soviet Union detonated its first atomic bomb. It is
difficult now to remember how shocked the United States government
was that its atomic secrets were no longer secret. The argument and
acrimony about developing a super weapon, the so-called hydrogen
bomb, ended on November 1, 1952, with the successful detonation of
the first truly thermonuclear weapon, the Ivy Mike Test, which totally
erased the island of Elugelab from the Eniwetok group.

The enormous pressure the Congressional Joint Committee on
Atomic Energy exerted on the Atomic Energy Commission to increase
the nuclear weapons stockpile was a crucial point in the curious history
of waste management. The people responsible for operations continu-
ally came up with ingenious plans for proper long-term care of nuclear
waste, but their proposals always became victims of higher priorities.
To accomplish anything in the federal government, one needs congressional authorization and the appropriation of funds. Without them,
little can happen. And little did.

In 1968, the General Accounting Office recommended a vigorous long-term waste management program, including an office within the AEC for policymaking and oversight. In response, an AEC task force made a number of recommendations and set up the office. But it wasn't until the much publicized leak at Hanford in 1973 that waste management rose to the front rank of nuclear concerns.

During the 1960s, the major effort in nuclear science turned away from military applications toward the production of isotopes and the transfer of that technology into the private sector; the development of nuclear medicine; the uses of radioactivity in industry, agriculture, physics, chemistry, biology, and geology; and the production of nuclear-generated electricity. All of these activities produce waste, some of it high level and very hazardous, but much of it with extremely low but detectable levels of radioactivity.

The AEC and later the Department of Energy (DOE) required that radioactive wastes be controlled according to explicit federal rules. Wastes were identified in three categories, low level (LLW), high level (HLW), and transuranic (TRU). The latter includes wastes, whether low level or high, that contain elements heavier than uranium (hence the name "transuranic") in amounts greater than 100 nanocuries per gram.

We will consider each of these categories separately, starting with low level wastes that account for only one percent of the radioactivity—but 99 percent of the volume—of all radioactive wastes. [5]

Low level wastes are those with an activity below 0.01 curies per kilogram. That's about *one billion* times less than the radioactivity in high level wastes. LLW comes mainly from industrial activities—for example, nondestructive testing, which, together with medical waste and that resulting from academic and research uses, accounts for about 43 percent, by volume, of radioactive waste. The remaining 56 percent (by volume) comes from nuclear power plants, and it includes the solidified radioactive nuclides removed from cooling water, protective clothing, and cleanup materials.

Regardless of source, all low level wastes are *solid* or must be solidified and appropriately packaged before being sent to a storage site. Three such sites have been in use for many years, one in South Carolina, another in Nevada, and a third in Washington State. In each case, the containers of LLW are inspected, monitored, and placed in shallow burial pits or trenches. They are not "dumped," a term critics persist in using. New LLW disposal sites are being constructed in California, Nebraska, New England, Illinois, and the Southwest, under a law that allows states to form cooperative compacts to take care of their low level waste and hence reduce its transportation.

Like most laws, the rules regarding LLW include some amusing anomalies. Certain radioactive products are exempt. Smoke detectors, for example, do not have to be sent to a repository, although their operation depends upon americium. Luminescent dials, watches, clocks, and instruments from planes, all of which generally contain tritium, and a product long on the American market, Coleman lanterns, whose mantles contain thorium, are exempt. Yet in the field of nuclear medicine, everything—injection needles, tubing, plastic and glass containers, swabs, gloves, even medical gowns that may come into contact with some isotope—is considered radioactive waste. Consider that in being tested or treated for a thyroid problem, 99 percent of the radioactive Iodine 131 goes into the patient's body; the remaining one percent remains trapped inside the needle or tubing and becomes low level waste. Iodine 131 has a half-life of eight days; it does not stay inside the patient, but is excreted in the normal manner. The patient is not required to void into a special container until all the radioactivity can be accounted for. It goes into the public sewage system, where it becomes greatly diluted and does no harm at all. Moreover, the human body itself contains radioactivity—about 0.1 microcuries of Potassium-40 and 0.1 microcuries of Carbon-14. According to the rules covering low level waste, that amount should mean that people cannot be buried, cremated, or disposed of in garbage. But, of course, the rule doesn't apply to humans—only to laboratory animals and to any material into which humans may put minute and harmless amounts of radioactivity.[6]

Finally, some waste that contains small amounts of radioactivity falls outside the laws governing radioactive waste, simply because it arises from activities that are not considered "nuclear." Burning coal is one of these—and remember that there are five million pounds of coal waste for every one pound of nuclear waste. In that regard, Walter Marshall, Lord Marshall of Goring and chairman of Britain's Central Electricity Generating Board, said in 1988:[7]

> Earlier this year, British Nuclear Fuels released into the Irish Sea some 400 kilograms of uranium, with the full knowledge of the regulators. This attracted considerable media attention and, I believe, some 14 parliamentary questions.
>
> I have to inform you that yesterday the C.E.G.B. released about 300 kilograms of radioactive uranium, together with all of its radioactive decay products, into the environment. Furthermore, we released some 300 kilograms of uranium the day before that. We shall be releasing the same amount of uranium today, and we plan to do the same tomorrow. In fact, we do it every day of every year so long as we burn coal in our power stations. And we do not call that "radioactive waste." We call it coal ash.

The same thing happens in the United States and throughout the world. Of all industries, the nuclear industry alone has taken responsibility for its wastes from the beginning. Yet, ironically, since no one has ever been hurt or contaminated, it is the one industry most often criticized for its waste management practices.

Transuranic Waste

Transuranic (TRU) waste is defined as waste that is contaminated with alpha-emitting radionuclides of atomic number greater than 92 and half-lives greater than 20 years (primarily plutonium) in concentrations greater than 100 nanocuries per gram (nCi/g). It is destined for geologic repository disposal. It decays primarily through the emission of alpha particles, which have short range, generate little heat, and are readily blocked. Radioactive waste with less than 100 nCi/g of TRU is, in effect, low level waste and disposed of in near-surface facilities, as appropriate. TRU waste must meet rigorous acceptance criteria (and sometimes processing) before it is ready for transportation and repository disposal.

Transuranic elements do not occur naturally; these wastes are produced mainly, though not exclusively, in the military nuclear programs. They are separated during the reprocessing of spent reactor fuel from the Navy and during reprocessing to obtain weapons-grade plutonium produced in special "production" reactors. Most TRU waste is separated and stored at the Idaho National Engineering Laboratory near Idaho Falls and at the Hanford Reservation in Washington; both of these federal facilities have reprocessing programs for military materials. TRU wastes also come from military programs at other military production facilities.

As with other waste forms, a large amount of research data have been accumulated on how best to handle transuranics. Present policy requires that the TRU waste be incorporated into borosilicate glass, encapsuled in canisters of stainless steel ten feet high and one foot in diameter and weighing 1,000 pounds, and emplaced in deep geologic storage.

A large cavern has been excavated for this purpose in bedded salt 2,100 feet below the surface near Carlsbad, New Mexico. Called the Waste Isolation Pilot Program (WIPP), all of the preparatory work has long been completed, but opponents have been successful so far in preventing the use of the facility. Because a few drops of water (water of crystallization from the salt under pressure) have been found dripping from the ceiling of some of the mile-long drifts, anti-nuclear activists have raised alarms that the waste may be dissolved in ground water and somehow will reach the surface and get into food. How the moisture could destroy the waterproof stainless steel jacket and dissolve borosilicate glass is not explained by the anti-nuclear forces. Nor is it revealed that if all the water now flowing through the ground in that part of New Mexico were diverted through the salt formation, it would take one million years to wash all the salt out of the repository. It's also useful to remember that glass artifacts from ancient Babylon known to be at least 3,000 years old have spent that time in flowing river water without being eroded. Glass does not dissolve in water—even in salty water—and can with high probability maintain its integrity over millions of years.

Fears have also been raised about the possibility of accidents during transportation. In response to these fears, the State of New Mexico has demanded that new roads be constructed into the Carlsbad site.

Although all scientific evidence supports the safety of long-term (many centuries) isolation deep underground in our radioactive earth, opposition continues. Yet, if all nuclear waste were put into the ground, that would increase the amount of radioactivity in the top 2,000 feet of soil in the United States by only one part in ten million. Even so, this may not be the best way to handle TRU waste. There are, in fact, two very good alternatives.

First, scientists at the Argonne National Laboratory have synthesized an entirely new substance named CMPO (for octyl [phenyl]-N, N-diisobutylcarbamoyl-methylphosphine oxide), which is capable of selectively isolating transuranics from the rest of the nuclear waste.[8] Extraction can be accomplished in conjunction with both nitric and hydrochloric acid solutions. By removing the TRUs, the remaining waste falls under the definition of low level waste and hence is easier to handle and manage economically. The removed TRUs are by a factor of from 100 to 1,000 times less in volume and can be solidified and vitrified. This procedure could save billions of dollars in disposal costs.

Second, it has long been known that exposing radioactive atoms to intense bombardment by neutrons can cause reversion to the stable state. In other words, radioactive wastes can be rendered non-radioactive by treatment in a neutron-producing reactor. Such a design has now been developed. It is the Argonne National Laboratory's Integral Fast Reactor, which produces an abundance of fast neutrons.[9]

Good sense would dictate the early construction of this fast reactor for the purpose of "burning" waste. How much better to destroy the radioactivity than to bury it! But no one has accused United States nuclear policymakers of making decisions based on good science, favorable economics, or common sense.

High Level Waste

High level waste is the highly radioactive mixture of fission products and TRU that results from reprocessing spent nuclear fuel and that requires permanent isolation. The decay heat in such waste produces elevated temperatures if not dissipated. HLW is of concern because of the simultaneous presence of heat and some TRU radionuclides of high toxicity and long half-lives.[10]

Heat from fission product decay diminishes rapidly with time after irradiation and dissipates easily at or near the surface of the ground. Depth generally increases thermal insulation and long-term isolation. After about 600 years of decay, the heat generation of HLW is not of any serious consequence. As already observed, these high level wastes account for only one percent of the volume of all radioactive wastes but 99 percent of the radioactivity.

Civilian high level waste is spent fuel from commercial power plants—for example, the solid 12-foot-long fuel rods removed from nuclear reactors during refueling.[11] They are intensely radioactive and contain much of the original uranium, the plutonium that has been produced, long-lived fission products, such as Cesium-137 and Strontium-90, and a number of other radionuclides and fission products. Typically, bundles of spent fuel rods are stored in large pools of water on the nuclear power plant site, where they will gradually cool. After that, the present official policy is to place the spent fuel in casks in deep geological storage.[12]

But in the case of high level waste, too, this burial plan has led to intense opposition. Only in the United States, which once led the world in the beneficial use of nuclear technology, is there a danger that fear of nuclear waste and the hysteria engendered by misinformation may cause our great nation to turn its back on nuclear power.

The high level waste that is the spent fuel from commercial nuclear power plants has been studied extensively. Research shows that both heat and the penetrating gamma radiation can be drastically lowered by separating out the unburned uranium and removing plutonium, cesium, and strontium. This is done routinely from defense reactor wastes and from the spent fuel of Navy propulsion reactors. Removal of these four isotopes can reduce the thermal burden by 98 percent and the gamma flux by 97 percent.

Such treatment is called reprocessing. It dramatically alters the character of the waste and facilitates handling, interim storage, transportation, and ultimate disposal. After removal of the gamma emitters, the residual waste form is more stable, its long-term behavior is more predictable, and its environmental and safety attributes are enhanced appreciably.

The unburned uranium and the plutonium can be refabricated into new fuel for producing electricity. This is the plutonium recycle plan—and what better way to take care of plutonium? That was the policy adopted by the AEC from the very beginning of the commercialization of nuclear power. That policy was abruptly put aside by President Carter's ban on reprocessing. Certainly, we should be using and reusing these fissionable isotopes. Every other nation with nuclear power plants reprocesses its fuel or is planning to. Why is it that recycling is supported with almost religious fervor for every kind of waste, excepting only nuclear?

Some of the useful isotopes that can be removed from spent fuel have already been discussed. To that group we can add other byproducts belonging to the group known as "noble" metals. Platinum is one of that group. These rare noble metals play an essential role in modern communications and the electronics industry. They are strategic minerals, but we don't have significant deposits. We import 94 percent of our annual needs from countries that mine and refine them, and there are only two such countries, the U.S.S.R. and South Africa.

Platinum itself does not exist in appreciable quantities in spent fuel, but other fission-product metals, such as palladium and technetium, do and can substitute for it. For example, technetium can be used instead of platinum as a catalyst in refining hydrocarbon fuels. The combined quantity of platinum-family metals and technetium in U.S. nuclear waste by the year 2000 is estimated to be 50 to 100 million ounces. We need one to three million ounces annually.

Garbage is not always what it seems. Today's nuclear waste contains many of tomorrow's useful materials, from the americium that makes smoke detectors work to uranium that can be recovered and burned again to produce electricity. Nuclear waste can be mined, but only if we have the will and the courage to look at it as a resource first, and dispose of it only when there's no more good in it.

So why don't we reprocess spent fuel and recover the many useful radionuclides? The shortsighted and foolish decision of President Carter against reprocessing was just that, shortsighted and foolish. The decision was based on two mistaken beliefs: first, an obsession with plutonium, coupled with an exaggerated fear of proliferation (there *are* ways to protect special materials); and second, the naive notion that if the United States were to forgo the benefits of reprocessing, all other nations would follow our lead. This, of course, has been proved wrong. No presidential decision was ever more tragically wrong or brought worse consequences for nuclear science in general and for waste management in particular.

Although President Reagan removed President Carter's prohibition against reprocessing, most qualified observers consider that the decision came too late. Why? For three reasons:

1. Millions of dollars in private funds have already been lost on the Barnwell reprocessing plant, built but never used, and private industry is unwilling to take further risk. The operation would therefore have to be government-operated, or at least run by GOCO (government owned, contractor operated).

2. There is an extensive legal apparatus set up around nuclear waste and laws have been passed concerning the way high level waste should be handled. Parenthetically, we have a great capacity to make law (the legislative branch), but absolutely none to *unmake* laws.

3. Hundreds of people whose jobs depend on waste and scores of businesses and industries are committed to the present policy—no matter how stupid it is.

But we have reached an impasse with the plan to put spent fuel into deep geological repositories. State after state has adopted the not-in-my-backyard attitude, and it is becoming increasingly clear that *there won't be any storage site in the United States,* especially with the formidable legal weapons the opponents have—and will use. Three billion dollars have been spent on HLW deep geological disposal, with no site available yet. Also, the costs are soaring, as always happens when delays are experienced, so that reprocessing need no longer prove itself on economic grounds.

So where are we? With a new opportunity and a new challenge. Now is the time to review the whole nuclear waste question and ask again whether reprocessing is better than burial. Reprocessing makes sense—scientifically, technically, and, above all, environmentally. After reprocessing and removal of all the useful and beneficial isotopes, the residual waste, properly packaged, should be disposed of *in the ocean.*[13]

As with everything else in our modern technological world, sea disposal has its opponents, and they are vocal—but wrong. There are deserts in the sea as there are on land. There are some areas completely devoid of life, lacking even geological evidence that anything *ever* lived there. In contrast to what some well-meaning but poorly informed people think, the sea is not a homogeneous soup of living things. Even whales do not swim through the ocean's deserts. Professional oceanographers have conducted extensive research in the deep sea, far from land, in the desert areas, and they have determined that disposal of radioactive waste (and toxic and hazardous wastes, too) can safely be contained in the sub-sea bed.[14]

The oceans consist of 323 million cubic miles of sea water covering nearly three-quarters of the earth's surface; the oceans are deep—hundreds of square miles of the sea are deeper than the highest mountains on land; the volume of sea water is so great that the dilution factor and heat sink are almost beyond calculation; and sea water is not potable. Why do we insist on keeping our wastes on land—just over one-quarter of the earth's surface—and putting at risk the tiny one percent of water that is fresh and on which our lives depend? Is there something sacred about the sea?

The sea already contains from natural processes 400 billion curies (Ci) of Potassium-40, 100 million Ci of radium, and one billion Ci of

Uranium-238. The top inch of the sea floor contains several million Ci of uranium; the Mississippi River alone adds 363 Ci of this renewable resource every year, 190 in the water and 173 in the sediment.

Many marine organisms themselves receive tens of rems (not millirems) of radiation per year from Polonium-210, which, like plutonium, is an alpha emitter, and one type of shrimp gets an annual dose of 100 rems. This all happens naturally. (For humans, the National Radiation Protection Board has set a level of 0.5 rems a year for the public, and 5 rems a year for occupational exposure, of which not more than 3 rems are to be absorbed in any one quarter.) The high doses absorbed by marine life have been discovered relatively recently and are further evidence that the avid absorption of radionuclides by fish and shrimps is harmless.

The amount of low level wastes now dropped into the sea is on the order of 100,000 Ci, and with hundreds of billions of Ci already there naturally, this is, well, a drop in the ocean.

Certainly it is hardly enough to substantiate the charge by Greenpeace (quoting Jackson Davis, a biologist at the University of California, Santa Cruz) that sea disposal of nuclear waste would make "a sea so radioactive that it could not support algae . . . which produce up to half of the world's oxygen." The truth is that there is not enough radioactivity available in the whole world to threaten the algae. And, as for oxygen, there is an equilibrium in its production and consumption; no torrents of oxygen move from the sea to the land. Also, since the air *above* sea water contains 7,500 times more oxygen than is produced by the microscopic algae *in* the water, should all photosynthesis in the sea somehow mysteriously cease, the oxygen in the atmosphere would decrease by only about ten percent over the next one million years.

Moreover, such radioactivity as has been introduced into the sea is quickly scavenged by natural processes, removed from the water, and carried into deep sediments, where it is ultimately unavailable to marine life.

Perhaps most convincing are the real-world experiments carried out that show how quickly the ocean recovers from contamination. In the Marshall Islands in the Pacific Ocean, Eniwetok, the scene of 46 atomic explosions, was thoroughly contaminated with radioactivity. [15]

Most of it ended up in the lagoon, where marine food chains were soon nearly free of radioactivity and could be consumed in quantity. Not so the terrestrial plants and animals. Even now, more than 30 years later, coconuts, breadfruit, and other plants, as well as land crabs, a native favorite, are still too radioactive from Strontium-90 and Cesium-137 to be eaten regularly. In the sea, however, these radionuclides are diluted by the massive amounts of stable strontium, calcium, cesium, and potassium, and pose almost no threat in marine food chains, despite their great potency in terrestrial food chains.

If nuclear waste were deposited in the ocean, it would be vitrified with borosilicate glass; encased in stainless steel canisters; taken into the deep ocean, far from land, and dropped so that it would *penetrate* the soft bottom sediments to a depth of several meters. Or the disposal could be carried out in casks emplaced in holes drilled in the subsea bed. Congress, unfortunately, has precluded ocean subseabed disposal. So we are left with putting these materials where we live—on land.

One of the ludicrous results of this acquiescence to uninformed sentimentality about the ocean is that over-aged nuclear submarines, which could safely be sent into the muck of the deep ocean by the simple, inexpensive expedient of opening a sea cock in the proper deep-ocean locale, must now be barged up the Columbia River and buried on the Hanford Reservation—costing American taxpayers millions of dollars.

And so the plan, up until recently, was to spend many millions of dollars studying the geological stability and suitability as a final resting place for high level waste of basalt (the Hanford Reservation, Washington State), volcanic tuff (Yucca Mountain, Nevada), and bedded salt (Deaf County, Texas). Despite expenditures totalling more than $3 billion since 1982, there is still no site, and the likelihood is now that there will not be any. Both Washington and Texas took advantage of the foot-dragging and temporizing by the Department of Energy and mounted successful campaigns to oppose any repository within their borders. It didn't take Nevadans much time to follow suit, and I say, good for them! Land disposal does not make good sense, even though it would be perfectly safe.

Speaking as a marine biologist, I join the great majority of ocean scientists in maintaining that the ocean, the deep ocean—the *bottom* of the deep ocean—is the proper place for waste disposal, both nuclear and chemical.

Of course, reprocessing and sea disposal can be done, but some well known and respected scientists will say that it cannot. But then, some well known and respected scientists and notables in the past have said such things as these:

> There is no likelihood that man can ever tap the power of the atom.
> —Robert Milliken, Nobel Prize in Physics, 1923.

> The energy produced by the breaking down of the atom is a very poor kind of thing. Anyone who expects a source of power from the re-transformation of these atoms is talking nonsense.
> —Ernest Rutherford, British physicist, Nobel Prize in Chemistry, 1908.

> There has been a great deal said about a 3,000-mile rocket. In my opinion, such a thing is impossible . . . we can leave it out of our thinking.
> —Vannevar Bush, physicist, MIT, 1945 Nobel Laureate.

> There is no hope for the fanciful idea of reaching the moon, because of insurmountable barriers to escaping the earth's gravity.
> —Dr. F. R. Moulton, astronomer, University of Chicago, 1932.

> While theoretically and technically television may be possible, commercially and financially I consider it an impossibility, a development of which we need waste little time dreaming.
> —Lee de Forest, American radio pioneer, 1926.

> What, sir? You would make a ship sail against the wind and currents by lighting a bonfire under her deck? I pray you, excuse me. I have no time to listen to such nonsense.
> —Napoleon Bonaparte, speaking to Robert Fulton, American inventor.

With nuclear waste, it's just a question of doing what is right and what is best—scientifically, technically, and environmentally. It's time to act with courage to do what is right for the United States, as well.

Part Four

PARTING
THOUGHTS

Chapter 12

ENVIRONMENTALISM AND THE FUTURE

As WE APPROACH the twenty-first century, we're given more than ever to reflecting upon what our society is all about, what our country means, what modern civilization has achieved, and, most of all, what the future promises to bring.

Our nation, which, to me, is the greatest the human race has conceived, is just a bit more than 200 years old. We can expect an endless supply of problems; some people have doubts about our science, our technology, and the way we use our knowledge. We have some hopes and many fears. We must wonder a little about our age. How old are we, anyway?

Human society has been around a long time, but recorded history goes back only about 6,000 years. The earth has been around between four and five billion years, and every generation of human beings that lives on it thinks its problems are the worst and that humankind has never faced such difficulties before. Most of us believe that unless we solve our problems now, all will be lost.

It's sobering to dwell upon how long humans have survived in a frequently hostile environment. We don't have claws, talons, or fangs. We have no barbs or poison glands to protect ourselves. We don't even have any fur or feathers to keep us warm when the ambient temperature drops; indeed, in our birthday suits, we are ill-adapted to live anywhere, except in the rather warm tropics. Our eyesight is not so good as that of most birds; our hearing is less keen than that of almost all of the higher animals; and our sense of smell is nothing compared to that of most fish and mammals. We can be outrun on land and outswum in the seas.

Yet, with all these difficulties, we've made it somehow. We have managed to penetrate every ecological niche, and we are able to survive in every environmental climate and condition anywhere on earth.

No other species of higher life can do so. You don't find polar bears swimming in a tropical sea; cactus does not grow in a rain forest. Plants and animals have their own ecological and environmental niches, and they are restricted to them. What, then, are our advantages?

First, we have a brain—a brain the likes of which is not seen in any other higher animal. That brain is capable of abstract thought; that brain can solve problems. We have developed a means of communication through human language that so far exceeds communication among other animals as to be in a completely different category. We are learning a good deal more about animal language and animal communication, but to compare even that of the higher primates or of whales and dolphins to the language capabilities of human beings is to overlook the enormous diversity of expression, the implications and nuances of words in the thousands of languages that exist among human beings. Abstract thought and language lead to systematized thinking, which leads to learning, the highest activity human beings engage in.

Learning and teaching, the buildup of knowledge, the questioning of truth, the development of philosophical systems, the practical applications of ideas—these are the things that distinguish humans from all other living things. When we join thoughts, speech, and learning to the peculiar capability to walk on two legs—thus freeing our arms— and the development of dextrous hands, we have a physical form that is truly remarkable in the animal kingdom. These gifts give us the ability to manufacture tools and gadgets of all kinds. They give us the ability to create engines and machines that utilize non-living energy, making the muscle power of slaves and beasts of burden unnecessary in modern society.

It is through our technology that we have been able to fly far away from earth to learn, in truth, how precious it is. It is no coincidence that our awakening to the special nature of our world and to its uniquely balanced environment and its limitations coincided with our first glimpse of earth from outer space, through the eyes of astronauts, television cameras, and photographic equipment. It was through technology that we saw ourselves as we really are, alone on one living, precious globe in space, a human family dependent on the resources of our minds and of our home planet, Earth.

Considering what we humans have accomplished, what we've done to build the modern high-tech society in which we live, and how we've swarmed across the land and changed its face—at least in the temperate region—some critics appear to be fearful that we are now about to destroy nature itself.

Are they right?

Without doubt, humans have been hard on the environment in many discrete places. Whenever mankind has cleared land to build a city or to farm or to manufacture something, the naturalness of nature has been changed. From a longer perspective, civilizations have come and gone since antiquity. Sometimes, in areas that were once inhabited and then abandoned, nature has taken over. On a shorter time scale, it has been demonstrated again and again that areas once despoiled by pollutants can return to being a healthy abode for many species.

True, humans can be and have been destructive, but humans also learn. The ways to live in harmony with nature while maintaining a comfortable, even high-tech, lifestyle are far better understood today. And more and more they are being practiced. There is no reason to believe that, inevitably, everything will get worse.

But activist environmentalists charge that man has gone beyond having an effect on the immediate vicinity of his activities and is now damaging the entire planet. They say man's industrial activities are changing the composition of the atmosphere, presumably irreversibly, through increased production of CO_2 and other greenhouse gases. As already pointed out, until the predictions of human-caused, global atmospheric alterations can be accepted as certain, there must be a satisfactory explanation for the increases in greenhouse gases 300 years ago, 150,000 years ago, and in the geological past. And it must be established that the ozone-destroying chloride ion really does, in fact, come from CFC and not from any of a number of natural sources.

In the light of the enormous size of the atmosphere and the hydrosphere, and the colossal natural forces involved, it would appear that man's puny activities are being vastly exaggerated. [1]

The fact is that weather will be what it is and that man's influence, if any, is trivial and relatively local. In the long term, climates, too, will change, as they have done in the past, determined not by man but by immense natural forces. Neither the sun nor the earth is immortal. Each will grow old and die. Inevitably, the sun will burn itself out, slipping first into that stage called a "red giant," where its size will become so huge that it will encompass the inner planets. Our earth will be swallowed up and cease to exist. Fortunately for us, the time scale for this is fairly long—about two billion years or so from now. That gives us a pretty good cushion of time to become better stewards of the environment. We are not ever going to control it on a worldwide scale.

Still, there are those who believe that we are threatening earth with intolerable stresses, born of just exactly those same things that have made us unique—human knowledge and technology. This belief finds expression in the modern environmental movement.

Now, aside from unrivaled success in obtaining favorable publicity for its positions, how is it that environmentalism became so successful? Part of the answer is fairly clear. There were two essential ingredients. One was national legislation that gave the activists access to the federal courts and standing before the law (the National Environmental Protection Act). In the last 15 years, more than 100 environmental laws have been passed. The other was the creation of many governmental agencies, including the Environmental Protection Agency, the Occupational Safety and Health Administration (OSHA), and the Nuclear Regulatory Commission.

Environmentalism, as we have come to know it in the waning years of the twentieth century, is a new and complex phenomenon.[2] It is new in the sense that it goes far beyond the traditional conservation movement—be kind to animals, support good stewardship of the earth, and so on—a philosophy of nature that we have known from the past. It is complex in that it incorporates a strongly negative element of anti-development, anti-progress, anti-technology, anti-business, anti-established institutions, and, above all, anti-capitalism.[3] Its positive side, if that is what it can be called, is that it seeks development of a society totally devoid of industry and technology.

As a movement, it is activist, adversarial, punitive, and coercive. It is quick to resort to force, generally through the courts or through legislation, although some of its more zealous adherents engage in physical violence (Earth First! and Greenpeace, for example). Finally, the environmentalist movement today has an agenda that goes far beyond a mere concern for nature, as shown by its links to and common cause with other leftist radical movements—such as are incorporated in the Green parties of Europe.

This is not to suggest that everyone who supports more responsible policies for cleaner air and water, who believes in restraining pollution, and who cares about how the earth's resources are used is a wild-eyed extremist. Far from it. The great majority of those who make up the membership of the Audubon Society, Sierra Club, National Wildlife Federation, Wilderness Society, Nature Conservancy, and countless other groups are fine, decent citizens. They are honest, honorable supporters of a good, clean environment and responsible human actions. However, the leaders of some of their organizations—such as the Natural Resources Defense Council, Friends of the Earth, Earth First!, Greenpeace, Government Accountability Project, Institute for Policy Studies, and many others—are determinedly leftist, radical, and dedicated to blocking industrial progress and unraveling industrial society.

These activist leaders and spokesmen are referred to as "political environmentalists" to distinguish them from the rest of us, who believe that using scientific data, not scare tactics, is the correct way to deal with environmental issues.

Modern environmentalism arose in response to real and widely recognized problems, among them: growing human pressures on natural resources, accumulation of wastes, and increased pollution of land, air, and water. Remember, for example, accounts from Cleveland about the alarming condition of the Cuyahoga River, which flows through the heart of Cleveland's industrial corridor into Lake Erie and was once called the world's most polluted river. So many gallons of industrial and chemical waste, oil, and other flammables had been dumped into it over the years that the river actually caught fire and blazed for a time. The Cuyahoga has since been cleaned up, and so has Lake Erie.

Without question, by the 1960s it was time to curb the excesses of a throwaway society. It was time to face up to the fact that there simply wasn't any "away" to throw things any more; "vacant" land and open space were limited. It was also time to recognize that there is a human tendency to overuse a good product, whether it's a vitamin, antibiotic, fertilizer, pesticide, or wilderness. It was time to redress many environmental wrongs. But, perhaps inevitably, the movement has gone beyond correcting past abuses and now poses real obstacles to industrial and technological progress.[4]

Under the slogan of protecting the environment, political environmentalists now oppose and cause delay in the construction of important facilities, even those that are obviously necessary and have wide support. It is now next to impossible and certainly far more expensive than in the past to build a sewage treatment plant, garbage incinerators, a power plant, a dam, or to open a new landfill. Industrial facilities, even when they are expected to produce useful commodities, hardly fare better. Liability for anything that might go wrong and the threat of litigation are effective deterrents used by political environmentalists against industry.

After achieving so much—establishing government agencies with oversight authority and regulatory power, armed with such laws as the National Environmental Protection Act, the Clean Air Act, the Clean Water Act, the Waste Management Act, and more than 100 other environmental laws—environmentalist groups apparently cannot leave well enough alone. They seem to be unable to let these laws and statutory agencies work to continue the significant progress of the last two decades. Instead, they press for ever more stringent and punitive controls. They continue to push for and insist on an unachievable pristine perfection, whatever the cost. Never mind that humans never survived without altering nature.

It is a fact that effluents no longer pour unchecked from the stacks and chimneys and waste pipes of industry. Open hearth furnaces and other industrial processes that depend on burning fuel have been largely replaced by electric furnaces and much of our foundry and smelting capacity has been shut down. Open burning of garbage no longer occurs and discharge of untreated sewage and waste water is becoming rare. It is certainly illegal.

Responsible timber companies have revised their logging practices and more trees are growing now than 50 years ago, an increase of more than three and a half times since 1920. Reforestation is a usual, not an occasional, practice. Coupled with modern agricultural procedures that require less land for food production, we now have at least as much wooded and forested acreage in America as existed in Colonial times, and probably more.

So what do the political environmental extremists want? Instant ecological perfection? A return to the Garden of Eden? To be in control? To exercise power? To remake society according to their political philosophy?

Activist environmentalists are mostly white, middle to upper income, and predominantly college-educated. They are distinguished by a vocal do-good mentality that sometimes successfully cloaks their strong streak of elitism, which is often coupled with a belief that the end justifies the means and that violence and coercion are appropriate tactics. Political environmentalists are adept at publicizing their causes, at exerting pressure on elected officials and government agencies, and at using the courts of law to achieve their aims.

They also tend to believe that nature is sacred and that technology is a sacrilege. Some environmentalists appear to be in favor of taking mankind back to pantheism or animism.

The idea that nature is "pure" and the almost religious awe with which it is held seems to be a part of the attraction, the drawing power of the movement. This attitude appears to permeate the thinking of a great many persons who are members of the Sierra Club, Audubon Society, Wilderness Society, Friends of the Earth, and other groups. We can look upon it as a very sincere, if somewhat sophomoric, emotional response to legitimate worries about the environment.

The leaders of the political environmentalists compound this reverence for the purity of nature with scare stories of looming man-made catastrophe. They say that our environmental problems are so serious as to threaten the continuation of life on Earth—or, if that's not true, that we should at least pretend that it is. But let their own words speak for them:

> Stewart Brand, writing in the *Whole Earth Catalogue*: "We have wished, we ecofreaks, for a disaster or for a social change to come and bomb us into the Stone Age, where we might live like Indians in our valley, with our localism, our appropriate technology, our gardens, our homemade religion—guilt-free at last!"[5]

> David Foreman, author of *A Field Guide to Monkey Wrenching* and founder of Earth First!: "We must . . . reclaim the roads and the plowed land, halt dam construction, tear down existing dams, free shackled rivers, and return to wilderness millions and tens of millions of [acres of] presently settled land."[6]

David Foreman is also the author of *Ecodefense*, now in its second edition and third printing. It features detailed, field-tested hints from experts on decommissioning heavy equipment, closing roads, stopping off-road vehicles, spiking trees, removing survey lines, hassling overgrazers, felling billboards, removing traplines, and much more!

> From the group, Ecotage, an offshoot of Earth First!: "We must make this an insecure and uninhabitable place for capitalists and their projects. This is the best contribution we can make towards protecting the earth and struggling for a liberating society."[7]

> Paul Watson, founder of Greenpeace: "I got the impression that instead of going out to shoot birds, I should go out and shoot the kids who shoot birds."[8]

Thomas Lovejoy, tropical biologist and assistant secretary of the Smithsonian Institution: "The planet is about to break out with fever, indeed it may already have, and we [human beings] are the disease. We should be at war with ourselves and our lifestyles."[9]

Jonathan Schell, author of *Our Fragile Earth*: "Now, in a widening sphere of decisions, the costs of error are so exorbitant that we need to act on theory alone, which is to say on prediction alone. It follows that the reputation of scientific prediction needs to be enhanced. But that can happen, paradoxically, only if scientists disavow the certainty and precision that they normally insist on. Above all, we need to learn to act decisively to forestall predicted perils, even while knowing that they may never materialize. We must take action, in a manner of speaking, to preserve our ignorance. There are perils that we can be certain of avoiding only at the cost of never knowing with certainty that they were real."[10]

Richard Benedick, an employee from the State Department working on assignment for the Conservation Foundation: "A global climate treaty must be implemented even if there is no scientific evidence to back the greenhouse effect."[11]

Stephen Schneider, proponent of the theory that CFCs are depleting the ozone: "[W]e have to offer up scary scenarios, make simplified, dramatic statements, and make little mention of any doubts we may have. Each of us has to decide what the right balance is between being effective and being honest."[12]

A spokesman for the Government Accountability Project, an offshoot of the Institute for Policy Studies (IPS): "Let's face it. We don't want safe nuclear power plants. We want NO nuclear power plants."[13]

Helen Caldicott, Australian pediatrician, speaking for the Union of Concerned Scientists: "Scientists who work for nuclear power or nuclear energy have sold their soul to the devil. They are either dumb, stupid, or highly compromised. . . . Free enterprise really means rich people get richer. And they have the freedom to exploit and psychologically rape their fellow human beings in the process. . . . Capitalism is destroying the earth. Cuba is a wonderful country. What Castro's done is superb."[14]

Paul Ehrlich, Stanford University biologist: "We've already had too much economic growth in the United States. Economic growth in rich countries like ours is the disease, not the cure."[15]

Paul Ehrlich deserves special attention, because his views sum up the anti-human trends of political-environmentalist thought—trends that frequently manifest themselves in predictions of global famine or plans for draconian measures to halt or reverse population growth. In *The Population Bomb*, Ehrlich predicted that the "battle to feed humanity is over. In the 1970s, the world will undergo famines. Hundreds of millions of people are going to starve to death in spite of any crash programs embarked upon now. Population control is the only answer."

Of course, that inevitable mass starvation didn't happen unless you were unlucky enough to have it imposed upon you by a Communist government in Ethiopia. But Ehrlich has persisted in his predictions. He predicted global famine in 1985, and was wrong. Now he says that the population of the United States will shrink from 250 million to about 22.5 million before 1999, because of famine and global warming.

He still recommends reducing population by force, saying: "Several coercive proposals deserve serious consideration, mainly because we will ultimately have to resort to them, unless current trends in birth rates are revised." Among Ehrlich's "coercive proposals" for the United States are deindustrialization, liberalized abortion, and tax breaks for people who have themselves sterilized. Ehrlich has many supporters in the environmental movement.

Kenneth Boulding, originator of the "Spaceship Earth" concept: "The right to have children should be a marketable commodity, bought and traded by individuals but absolutely limited by the state."[16]

From the Earth First! newsletter: "If radical environmentalists were to invent a disease to bring human populations back to sanity, it would probably be something like AIDS. It [AIDS] has the potential to end industrialism, which is the main force behind the environmental crises."[17]

More from David Brower of Friends of the Earth: "Childbearing [should be] a punishable crime against society, unless the parents hold a government license. . . . All potential parents [should be] required to use contraceptive chemicals, the government issuing antidotes to citizens chosen for childbearing."

Brower believes "other people's children" constitute pollution and are therefore an environmental concern. [18]

But enough. The common threads of belief that seem to run through these opinions are Malthusian ideas of finite resources, limits to growth, forced population control, a distrust of human beings, a belief in the omnipotence of the State and its ability to control individual choice, and a rejection of science, technology, and industrialization. Does this represent the convictions of most Americans? No way!

Although I have focused on home-grown environmentalists, the same attitudes can be found abroad, as well. Prince Philip of the United Kingdom, leader of the World Wildlife Fund, stated recently that, were he to be reincarnated, he would wish to return as a "killer virus to lower human population levels." [19] Clearly, his royal highness is not fond of people. In its annual report, the World Wildlife Fund laid out its goals, and included this statement: "Increasing [human] population causes a drain on natural resources, which is geometric, not arithmetic. . . . Science cannot be expected to supplant the vital processes of nature."

On December 28, 1988, the respected London weekly *The Economist*, editorialized: "The extinction of the human species may not only be inevitable, but a good thing. . . . This is not to say that the rise of human civilization is insignificant, but there is no way of showing that it will be much help to the world in the long run." [20]

Speaking for the Green Party of West Germany, Carl Amery has said: "We, in the Green movement, aspire to a cultural model in which the killing of a forest will be considered more contemptible and more criminal than the sale of 6-year-old children to Asian brothels." [21] Nice guy, Amery.

Ecoemotion and hysteria has also, of course, many adherents in Congress. Writing in *The International Herald-Tribune* under the title,

"The Environment Indicts Our Civilization," Senator Albert Gore of Tennessee anticipates what he calls "an environmental holocaust without precedent."[22]

If this were just political rhetoric, it could be dismissed. But Gore is serious. He calls for a series of global summit meetings to seek the "unprecedented international cooperation that the environmental crisis will demand."

Gore is supported by Frederico Mayor Zaragoza, director general of UNESCO, who said in Belgium in March 1989, that "the environment has to be addressed through global measures, but you need ways of enforcing them." The "ways" would be through a uniformed and armed United Nations "green force" equivalent to the blue-helmeted UN military peacekeeping force.[23]

Senator Gore is not alone in his radical environmental stand. He is joined by many of his colleagues, including Senator Timothy Wirth of Colorado and Representative Claudine Schneider of Rhode Island. Representative Schneider has introduced a bill titled "Global Warming Prevention Act of 1989." It orders the United States government to take extensive tracts of land out of food production and cultivate sugar cane for ethanol to replace gasoline. On the international level, the Schneider bill calls for cutting off all aid to countries that propose any development other than those using "least-cost energy." It also directs that "priority shall be given to programs that enhance access of the poor to low-cost vehicles and efficient carrying devices, including access to credit for the purchase of bicycles, carts, pack animals, and similar affordable, non-motorized vehicles."[24] How many citizens would agree that our tax money should be used to purchase draft animals?

We could hope that other members of Congress do not share this kind of environmental insanity, but 49 senators are co-sponsors on the bills introduced by Gore, Wirth, and Schneider.

Vermont Senators Leahy and Jeffords have a detailed piece of legislation, S–333, that declares, grandly, "the Congress, recognizing the profound, irreversible, and potentially catastrophic impacts of humanity's activities on the global atmosphere and the world's environment and the inability of science to predict with certainty the consequences for humanity of any such changes, hereby declares that each person has a responsibility and obligation to avoid contamination of the atmosphere."[25]

That's nice, but what can the common, everyday, sensible, taxpaying citizen do? Here are some suggestions:

First, a person can put pressure, individually and through groups, on members of the legislative branch, both state and federal, to refrain from acting precipitously on expensive "cures" for unproven environmental ills. Ask for evidence. It's public tax money that they are proposing to spend; it should not be wasted.

Second, don't succumb to the argument put forward by political environmentalists that action must be taken in advance of understanding the problem, "just in case." Keep in mind that they have a job or position to protect. Remember, the alarmists depend on continued crises, even if they are contrived, to keep themselves in business. Insist on facts.

Third, keep a sense of perspective. This old earth has been through a lot, including drastic climate changes, without any help from humans. It will continue to change. The earth has never been stable or remained the same for long.

Finally, humans cannot live on earth without altering it and without using natural resources. Our responsibility is to be good stewards of the environment and to remember that a well-tended garden is better than a neglected woodlot. It is demeaning beyond belief to consider mankind simply another species of animal, no better and no worse than wild beasts.

We human beings are what we are—imperfect but well-meaning and capable of improvement. We learn from mistakes. We have the ability to think rationally; and we should do so more often. We also have the gift to make conscious choices; and we should choose to pursue knowledge and understanding that will better the lot of all species on the planet.

In Goethe's *Faust*, Faust, jaded with every conceivable worldly experience, finally finds, in a land reclamation project, the contentment that has eluded him all his life.[26]

Now it may seem strange that Faust should find his greatest happiness in a prosaic engineering project. But in nineteenth century Europe, the clearing of swamps had clear human benefits. (Swamps had not been graduated to the status of "wetlands," and no environmental impact studies were required.) Faust's soul was saved, not because he reclaimed land, but because, in Goethe's immortal words, "whosoever, aspiring, struggles on, for him there is salvation."

In this sense and in the knowledge that we who believe in technology are engaged in the struggle to improve the lot of every human being, we can still share Goethe's enthusiasm and have a taste of Faust's salvation.

END NOTES

Preface:
(1) Mischler, Norman, 1977. The parable repeated here first appeared in *The London Sunday Times*, 27 March 1977.

Chapter 1:   WHO SPEAKS FOR SCIENCE?

(1) This chapter, revised and updated, is based on a speech bearing the same title that I gave at the Pacific Northwest Shavano Institute Seminar sponsored by Hillsdale College and printed in *Imprimis*, Vol. 17, No. 8, August 1988.

(2) *The Morning News Tribune*, Tacoma, p. 1, 23 February 1988.

(3) Ray, Dixy Lee, 1988, "Who Speaks for Science?", *Imprimis*, Vol. 17, No. 8, August 1988, Hillsdale College, Hillsdale, MI 49242.

* Golden, William T., editor, 1988, *Science and Technology: Advice to the President, Congress, and Judiciary*, Permagon Press, Maxwell House, Fairview Park, Elmsford, NY 10523.

* Beckmann, Petr, 1986, "The War on Nuclear Energy: The Edge We Give to Pseudoscience," *World Media Report*, Vol. 1, No. 1, pp. 1–8.

* Isaac, Rael Jean and Erich Isaac, 1985, *The Coercive Utopians*, p. 256, Discipleship Books, Regnery Gateway, Inc., 1130 17th St., Washington, DC 20036.

(4) Whelan, Elizabeth, 1985, *Toxic Terror*, Jameson Books, Inc., 722 Columbus Street, Ottawa, IL 61350.

(5) Efron, Edith, 1984, *The Apocalyptics*, Simon & Schuster, Rockefeller Center, 1230 Avenue of the Americas, NY 10020.

(6) Ray, Dixy Lee, 1988, op. cit., "Who Speaks for Science?"

(7) Beckmann, Petr, 1985, *The Health Hazards of NOT Going Nuclear*, Golem Press, Box 1342, Boulder, CO 80306, original printing 1979.

* Beckmann, Petr, 1982, *Doctors Against Health*, Golem Press, Box 1342, Boulder CO 80306.

(8) Lindzen, Richard S., 1990, "Some Coolness Regarding Global Warning," *Journal of the American Meteorological Society*, Vol. 71, No. 3, March 1990.

(9) Arnold, Ron, 1986, "Media Coverage of the Environment," *World Media Report*, Vol. 1, Nos. 2 and 3.

(10) Kemeny, John G., 1980, "Saving American Democracy: The Lessons of Three Mile Island," *Technology Review*, June/July, pp. 65–75.

(11) For many of the thoughts presented here and for the term, "factoids," I am indebted to the article, "The Different Worlds of Scientists and Reporters," by G. I. Baskerville and K. L. Brown, published in the University of New Brunswick's "Forestry Focus," and reprinted in the *Journal of Forestry*. See also the editorial, "Who Speaks for Science?" by Dr. Alan Moghissi, published in *Environment International*, Vol. 13, pp. 231–233, 1987.

(12) Efron, Edith, 1984, *The Apocalyptics*, op. cit.

(13) Kelly, Judge Patrick, 1984, Opinion in *Johnston vs. the United States*, U.S. District Court, Kansas, 1984, in Federal Supplement, Vol. 597, pp. 374–434.

Chapter 2   THE GOOD OLD DAYS?

(1) All statements are from personal recollection. Similar reminiscences can be found in:

* Luce, Ambassador Claire Boothe, 1987, *World Media Report*, Vol. 1, No. 4, pp. 217–221.

* Tucker, William, 1982, *Progress and Privilege: America in the Age of Environmentalism*, Chapter 9, "Pages From Environmental History," Anchor Press/Doubleday, Garden City, NY.

* Borlaug, Norman, 1985, in the Foreword to *Toxic Terror*, op. cit.

Chapter 3   IT WORKS BETTER IF YOU PLUG IT IN

(1) Tucker, William, 1982, *Progress and Privilege*, op. cit., p. 228ff.

(2) Schurr, Sam H., and Sidney Sonenblum, 1986, *Electricity Use, Productive Efficiency and Economic Growth*. Electrical Power Research Institute, 3412 Hillview Avenue, Palo Alto, CA 94304.

(3) Edison, Thomas A., 1984, in *He Illuminated the Path of Progress*, Ascent, Atomic Energy Canada, Ltd., (AECL), 1984 Spring, pp. 8–13.

(4) Beckmann, Petr, 1978, *Pages From U.S. History*, Golem Press, op. cit., pp. 1–15.

(5) Mills, Mark P., 1987, *Implications of Recent Trends in Industrial Electrification*, Science Concepts: USCEA, 1776 I Street, NW, Suite 400, Washington, DC 20006.

* Beckmann, Petr, 1988, "New England Power Pool Problems," in *Access to Energy*, Vol. 16, No. 2, October 1988.

* *The Rise of Electric Steelmaking*, EPRI Journal, op. cit., April/May 1988.

(6) NERC report, 1989, North American Electricity Reliability Council, 101 College Road East, Princeton, NJ 08540.

* Navarro, Peter, 1982, "Our Stake in the Electric Utilities' Dilemma," *Harvard Business Review*, No. 82311, May/June 1982.

* Myers, Richard, 1988, "Future Shock: The Need for Power," *Nuclear Industry*, March/April 1988, pp. 22–30.

* Warren, Anita, 1989, "That Powerless Feeling," *Nuclear Industry*, first quarter 1989.

* Wargo, J. R., 1988, "The New Fad: Tailoring Demand," *Nuclear Industry*, July/August 1988, pp. 41–48.

* Starr, Chauncey and Milton F. Searl, 1989, *Global Electricity Futures: Demand and Supply Alternatives*, EPRI reports, presented at ANS annual meeting, 27 November 1989.

* Mills, Mark et al, 1986, *A Return to the World of Oil?*, Science Concepts, Inc., U.S. Committee for Energy Awareness, March 1986.

Chapter 4:   GREENHOUSE EARTH

The recent literature on this contemporary issue is too voluminous to cover completely. Two of the more significant, critical contributions that offer a comprehensive review of the important problems are listed here. One is:

* *Global Climate Change: Human and Natural Influences*, edited by S. Fred Singer, 1989, Paragon House, 90 Fifth Avenue, NY 10001.

The other is:

* NAPAP, the National Acid Precipitation Assessment Program, 1990, by Director James Mahoney, a congressionally mandated ten-year study costing more than $500 million.

It is a pity—and a great financial burden to the American taxpayer—that Congress has carefully ignored both in the provisions of the 1990 Clean Air Act.

(1) Hansen, James E., 1988, *The Greenhouse Effect: Impacts on Current*

Global Temperatures and Regional Heat Waves, testimony given before the Senate Committee on Energy and Natural Resources, typewritten report.

(2) "Hansen vs. the World on the Greenhouse Effect," *Science*, Vol. 244, pp. 1041–43, 2 June 1989.

(3) Rediske, John, 1970, "Young Forests and Global Oxygen Supply," *Weyerhauser World*, Vol. 2, No. 4, April 1970.

(4) Sedjo, Roger and Marion Clausen (Resources for the Future), 1989, "Prices, Trade, and Forest Management," *Econ Update*, Reason Foundation, Vol. 3, No. 8, April 1989.

(5) Broecker, Wallace S. and George H. Denton, 1990, "What Drives Glacial Cycles," *Scientific American*, Vol. 262, No. 1, p. 48ff.

(6) *The 1980 Eruptions of Mount St. Helens*, Washington Geological Survey Professional Paper 1250, Peter W. Lipman and Donald R. Mullineaux, editors, 1981.

(7) Maxey, Margaret, 1985, *Technology and a Better Environment*, National Council for Environmental Balance, Inc., PO Box 7732, Louisville, KY 40207.

* Davies, John, 1986, "Public Safety vs. Augustine's Eruption: Augustine Erupts Again," *The Geophysical Institute Quarterly*, Vol. 4, No. 4, July 1986, University of Alaska, Fairbanks.

* Hefferich, Carla, 1990, "Review and Update of Redoubt's 'New Series' of Eruptions, Starting 13 December 1989," *The Geophysical Institute Quarterly*, Alaska, op. cit., Vol. 8, Nos. 1 and 2, Winter 1990 (The December 1989 plume equaled six miles; the biggest to date came on 2 June 1990—40,000 feet within 30 minutes.)

(8) Fitzgerald, Doreen, 1990, *Sun Meets Earth*, Vol. 8, Nos. 1 and 2.

(9) Douglas, John et al, 1989, "A Storm From the Sun," *EPRI Journal*, op. cit., July/August 1989.

(10) Eddy, John, 1982, "C-14 Radioactivity in Tree Rings," *Access to Energy*, Vol. 9, No. 7, March 1982, Box 2298, Boulder, CO 80306.

* Eddy, John, 1977, "The Case of the Missing Sunspots," *Scientific American*, 1977.

* Idso, Sherwood, 1989, CO_2 *and Global Change: Earth in Transition*, Institute for Biospheric Research, 631 East Laguna Drive, Tempe, AZ 85282.

(11) Nierenberg, William, Robert Jastrow, and Frederick Seitz, 1989, *Scientific Perspectives on the Greenhouse Problems*, George C. Marshall Institute, 11 DuPont Circle, No. 506, Washington, DC 20036.

* Nierenberg et al, "Global Warming: Blaming the Sun," *Science*, Vol. 246, No. 24, 1989.

* Maize, Kennedy, 1989, *Global Warming Science Flawed?*, Vol. 17, No. 109, 9 June 1990.

(12) Lindzen, Richard S., 1990, "Some Coolness Concerning Global Warming," *Journal of the American Meteorology Society*, Vol. 71, No. 3, March 1988.

* Shepard, Michael et al, 1988, "The Politics of Climate," *EPRI Journal*, op. cit., Vol. 13, No. 4, June 1988.

(13) Support for nuclear power comes not only from the U.S. Council on Energy Awareness—1988 Midyear Report: *Taking Another Look at Nuclear*, 23 June 1988—but also from

* White, Robert M., president of the National Academy of Engineering, in testimony before the Senate Committee on Commerce, Science, and Transportation, 13 July 1988, and a news release from Senator Tim Wirth, 18 July 1988.

(14) Ellsaessar, Hugh W., 1989, "A Review of the Scientific American Article: Managing Planet Earth," *20th Century Energy and Environment*, November/December 1989.

(15) Brookes, Warren T., "The Global Warming Panic," *Forbes*, 25 December 1989.

(16) Bentley, Charles R., 1990, "Recent Data From Measurements of Antarctic Glaciers," *Insight*, 15 January 1990.

(17) Hammitt, J. K., 1987, "Timing Regulations to Prevent Stratospheric Ozone Depletion," *Rand Report*, R-3495-JMO/RC, April 1987, pp. 42–43.

(18) Singer, S. Fred, 1989, "Stratospheric Ozone: Science and Policy," in *Global Climate Change: Human and Natural Influences*, S. Fred Singer, editor, Paragon House, 90 Fifth Avenue, NY.

* Singer, S. Fred, 1989, "My Adventures in the Ozone Layer," *National Review*, 30 June 1989.

* Maduro, Rogelio, 1989, "The Myth Behind the Ozone Hole Scare," *21st Century*, July/August 1989.

* Maduro, Rogelio, 1989, "The 'Greenhouse Effect' Hoax," *EIR Special Report, Executive Intelligence Review*, PO Box 17390, Washington, DC 20041.

(19) Report by the National Bureau of Standards, referenced in *Access to Energy*, April, 1989, Vol. 16, No. 8.

Further recommended reading:

* Ellsaesser, Hugh W., 1989, *Atmospheric Carbon Dioxide and the Climate Record*, Lawrence Livermore National Laboratory, UCRL-100954 Preprint, April 1989.

* Ausubel, Jesse and Asit K. Besivas, editors, 1980, *Climate Con-*

straints and Human Activities, Pergamon Press, Maxwell House, Fairview Park, Elmsford, NY 10523.

* Bach, W. et al, 1980, *Interactions of Energy and Climate*, D. Reidel Publishing Co., Dordrecht: Holland/Boston/London.

* Winkless, Nels III and Iben Browning, 1987, *Climate and the Affairs of Men*, Fraser Publishing, Box 494, Burlington, VT 05402.

* MacLeish, William H., 1989, "Painting a Portrait of the Gulf Stream From Miles Above—and Below," *Smithsonian*, Vol. 19, No. 12, March 1989.

* Weiner, Jonathan, 1989, "Glacier Bubbles Are Telling Us What Was in Ice Age Air," *Smithsonian*, Vol. 20, No. 2, May 1989.

* Moore, Taylor, 1989, "The Challenge of Doing Without CFCs," *EPRI Journal*, September 1989, op. cit.

* Moore, Taylor, 1989, "Concern Over Ozone," *EPRI Journal*, June 1989, op. cit.

* *Climate Through the Ages*, C. E. P. Brooks, NY, Dover Publishing, 1970.

* Special Issue (many authors), "The Struggle to Save Our Planet," *Discover*, Vol. 11, No. 4, April 1990, pp. 36–78.

* Ray, Dixy Lee, 1990, "Greenhouse Earth: The Facts About Global Warming," *Our Land*, Vol. 11, No. 1, Summer 1990, p. 12ff.

* "Precise Monitoring of Global Temperature Trends From Satellites," published in *Science* 30 March 1990 by R. W. Spencer and J. R. Christy shows that over a ten-year period (1979–88) there has been no discernible warming trend on earth.

It is worth noting that increasing numbers of scientists are coming to the conclusion that doubling the CO_2 concentration in the atmosphere and raising the global temperature by two degrees Centigrade would result in benefits that far outweigh any possible harm. Biologist Boyd Strain says, "We are moving from a carbon-starved world back to a carbon-fertilized world. Many agriculture scientists believe that the worldwide rise in food production during the last 40 years is due in part to increasing availability of CO_2." Consult *Carbon Dioxide and Climate Change*, by Sherwood Idso, for fascinating details.

Chapter 5: ACID RAIN

(1) Thomas, Lee M., 1986, "The Next Step: Acid Rain," *EPA Journal*, June/July 1986, pp. 2–3.

(2) Likens, G. E. et al, 1979, "Acid Rain," *Scientific American*, Vol. 241,

No. 4, pp. 43–51, October 1979, and numerous technical articles in professional journals.

(3) Smil, Vaclav, 1985, "Acid Rain: A Critical Review of Monitoring Baselines and Analyses," University of Manitoba, *Power Engineering*, pp. 59–63, April 1985.

(4) Tilling, R. I., M. Rubin et al, 1984, "Holocene Eruptive Activity of El Chicon Volcano," *Science*, 18 May 1984, pp. 747–749.

* Weiner, Jonathan, 1989, Glacial Air Bubbles Are Telling Us What Was in Ice Age Air, *Smithsonian*, Vol. 20, No. 2, May 1989, op. cit.

(5) *Acid Deposition in Atmospheric Processes in Eastern North America*, Environmental Sciences Board, National Research Council, National Academy Press, 1985.

(6) National Acid Precipitation Assessment Program, 1984, Annual Report to the President and Congress.

* National Acid Precipitation Assessment Program, 1990 Final Report (unpublished), see *Wall Street Journal* editorial, "No PAP From NAPAP," 26 January 1990.

* Mohnen, Volker A., 1988, "The Challenge of Acid Rain," *Scientific American*, Vol. 259, No. 2, August 1988.

* Boutacoff, David, 1988, "Reality Test for Acid Rain Models," *EPRI Journal*, op. cit., Vol. 13, No. 8, December 1988.

(7) Stumm, Werner, Laura Sigg, and Jerald L. Schnoor, 1987, "Aquatic Chemistry of Acid Deposition," *Environmental Science & Technology*, Vol. 21, No. 1, 1987.

* Gaffany, Jeffery S. et al, 1987, "Beyond Acid Rain," Los Alamos National Laboratory, *Environmental Science & Technology*, Vol. 21, No. 6, 1987.

* Henriksen, Arne and David F. Brakke, 1988, "Sulfate Deposition to Surface Waters," *Environmental Science & Technology*, Vol. 22, No. 1, 1988.

* Campbell, S. and M. Arlanskas, 1983, *Comparison of Sulfur and Nitrogen Oxide Emission Rates With Wet Deposition Rates in the State of Maryland*, Environmental Sciences Board, National Research Council, National Academy Press, 1983.

* Altshuller, Aubrey P. and R. A. Linthurst, editors, 1983, *The Acidic Deposition Phenomenon and Its Effects: Critical Assessment Review Papers*, EPA Document 600/8-83-016B, May 1983.

(8) *The 1980 Eruptions of Mount St. Helens*, Washington, op. cit., 1981.

* Landsberg, H. E., 1984, "Global Climate Trends" in *The Resourceful Earth*, edited by Julian L. Simon and Herman Kahn, Basil Blackwell,

Inc., 432 Park Avenue South, Suite 1505, NY 10016; for eruptions of El Chicon and other volcanoes, see pp. 288–289.

(9) Stoiber, R. B. and A. Jepsen, 1973, "SO$_2$ Contributions to the Atmosphere by Volcanoes," *Science*, Vol. 182, 1973.

(10) Landsberg, H. E., 1984, in *The Resourceful Earth*, op. cit.

* Whelan, Elizabeth, 1985, in *Toxic Terror*, Chapter 12, "Do the Acid Raindrops Keep Falling?," op. cit.

(11) Manion, Paul D. and R. J. Bragg, 1982, *Effects of Acid Precipitation on Scleroderris Canker Disease of Red Pine*, pp. 55–56, proceedings of NY State Symposium on Atmospheric Deposition, Center for Environmental Research, Cornell University, Ithaca, NY.

* Manion, Paul D. et al, *Air Pollutants' Effects on Forest Ecosystems*, Acid Rain Foundation symposium report, 1630 Blackhawk Hills, St. Paul, MN 55122.

(12) Kiester, Edwin J., 1985, "A Deathly Spell Is Hovering Above the Black Forest," *Smithsonian*, Vol. 16, No. 8, November 1985.

(13) McKetta, John J., Jr., 1985, *Acid Rain, What Is the Real Story? Effects on Lakes and Fish*, Department of Chemical Engineering, University of Texas, Austin 78712, distributed by the National Council for Environmental Balance, Louisville, KY 40207.

* McKetta, John J., Jr., 1987, *Acid Rain, The Whole Story to Date*, the National Council for Environmental Balance, Louisville, KY 40207.

* Schindler, D. W., 1988, "Effects of Acid Rain on Freshwater Ecosystems," *Science*, Vol. 239, 8 January 1988.

* Porcella, Donald, 1988, "Lake Acidification Mitigation," *EPRI Journal*, July/August 1988.

(14) Singer, S. Fred, 1984, "Acid Rain: A Billion Dollar Solution to a Million Dollar Problem," *Policy Review*, No. 27, Winter 1984.

(15) Ray, Dixy Lee, 1988, "Acid Rain: What to Do?", *Environmental Science & Technology*, Vol. 22, No. 4, 1988, p. 348.

(16) Historically, the following publications are important:

* Lewis, Drew and William Davis, *Joint Report of the Special Envoys on Acid Rain*, mimeo only, January 1986.

* 1986, various authors, *Acid Deposition: Long Term Trends*, Environmental Sciences Board, National Academy Press, 1986.

* Herrington, John S., 1986, testimony before House Committee on Energy and Resources on HR 4567, 20 June 1986, mimeo only.

* McCormick, John, 1989, second edition, *Acid Earth*, Earthscan Publications, Ltd., 3 Endsleigh Street, London, WC1 HOD. Although this

World Wildlife Fund book maintains a staunchly anti-SO_2 prejudice throughout, it also presents a wealth of interesting information on the SO_2 controversy in England and Scandinavia and on the situation in Southeastern Canada. It is remarkable that the author is able to relate political, social, religious, and economic problems—*everything*—to acid deposition!

For more information, consult the following:

1990:

* Krug, Edward C., 1990, "Fish Story: The Great Acid Rain Flimflam," *Policy Review*, Spring 1990, pp. 44–48.

1986:

* Various authors, *Acid Deposition: Long Term Trends*, Environmental Studies Board, National Research Council, National Academy Press, 1986.

* HR-4567, Status of Major Legislation, Weekly Bulletin, 21 July, 11 August, 14 August 1986.

1984:

* Quinn, Scott O., editor, *Acid Deposition, Trace Contaminants, and Their Indirect Health Effects, Research Needs*, Corvallis Environmental Research Laboratory, U.S. EPA, 200 SW 35th Street, Corvallis, OR 97333.

* Zurer, Pamela S., "Volcanoes, Nature's Caldrons," *Chemistry and Engineering News*, 24 September 1984.

* Nierenberg, William A., chairman, *Report of the Acid Rain Peer Review Panel*, mimeo copy, Office of Science and Technology Policy, July 1984.

1983:

* Interagency Task Force on Acid Precipitation, NAPAP, Annual Report, 1983.

* Munger and Eisenreich, *Environmental Science and Technology*, Vol. 17, pp. 32–42.

* Kramer and Tessier, *Environmental Science and Technology*, Vol. 16, pp. 606–615.

* Pruppacher, H. R. et al, *Precipitation Scavenging, Dry Deposition, and Resuspension, Vol. 1*, publication sponsored by EPA.

1982:

* Galloway et al, *Journal of Geophysical Research*, Vol. 87, pp. 8771–8786, 1982.

* Sequerea et al, *Journal of the Air Pollution Control Association*, Vol. 32, pp. 241–245.

1981:

* Committee on the Atmosphere and Biosphere, *Atmosphere-Biosphere*

Interactions: Toward A Better Understanding of the Ecological Consequences of Fossil Fuel Combustion, National Research Council, National Academy Press, 1981.

* Casadevall, Thomas J. et al, "SO_2 Emission Rates From Mount St. Helens, March/December 1981," in *The 1980 Eruptions of Mount St. Helens*, Geological Survey Professional Paper 1250, U.S. Government Printing Office.

* Hansen, D. A., G. M. Hidy, and G. J., Stensland, consultants, *Examination of the Basis for Trend Interpretation of the Historical Rain Chemistry in the Eastern U.S.*, Environmental Research and Technology, Inc., Document No. P.-A097, February 1981.

* Tyree et al, *Atmospheric Environment*, Vol. 15, pp. 57–60, 1981.
In addition, the following Journal reports have been consulted but not specifically quoted:

* Nguyen, B. C. et al, "The Role of the Ocean in the Global Atmospheric Sulfur Cycle," *Journal of Geophysical Research*, Vol. 88, No. C-15, pp. 10.903–10.914, 20 December 1983.

* Moller, Detlev, "Estimation of Global Man-Made Sulfur Emission," *Atmospheric Environment*, Vol. 18, No. 1, pp. 19–27, 1984.

* Andrcae, Meinrat O. and Hans Raemdouck, "Dimethyl Sulfide in the Surface Ocean and the Marine Atmospheres: A Global View," *Science*, Vol. 221, pp. 744–747, 19 August 1983.

* Aneja, Viney P., Arun P. Aneja, and Donald F. Adams, "Biogenic Sulfur Compounds and the Global Sulfur Cycle," *Journal of the Air Pollution Control Association*, Vol. 32, No. 8, pp. 803–807, August 1982.

* Rice, Herbert, D. H. Nochiamson, and G. M. Hidy, "Contribution of Anthropogenic and Natural Sources to Atmospheric Sulfur in Parts of the United States," *Atmospheric Environment*, Vol. 15, pp. 1–9, Pergamon Press, 1981.

* Cullis, C. F. and M. M. Hirschler, "Atmospheric Sulfur: Natural and Man-Made Sources," *Atmospheric Environment*, Vol. 14, pp. 1263–1278, 1980.

* Robinson, Elmer, and Robert C. Robbins, "Gaseous Sulfur Pollutants From Urban and Natural Sources," *Journal of the Air Pollution Control Association*, Vol. 20, No. 4, pp. 233–235, April 1970.
Including numerous issues of two energy newsletters:

* *Access to Energy*, publisher Petr Beckmann, Colorado Springs.
* *Energy Daily*, publisher Lewellen King, Washington, DC.

Chapter 6: "Acid Rain" for Insects: Pesticides

(1) Jukes, Thomas H., 1974, "Insecticides in Health, Agriculture and the Environment," *Naturwissenschaften*, Vol. 66, 1974.

* Jones, Pamela, 1989, *Pesticides and Food Safety*, American Council on Science and Health, 1995 Broadway, 16th floor, NY 10023.

(2) Claus, George and Karen Bolander, 1977, *Ecological Sanity*, David McKay, pp. 289–91.

* Jukes, Thomas H., 1988, "How to Survive When Everyone's Scared," *21st Century*, September/October 1988.

(3) Claus, George and Karen Bolander, op. cit., p. 294.

* Edwards, J. Gordon, 1983, *Saving Lives With Pesticides*, National Council for Environmental Balance, 4169 Westport Road, Louisville, KY 40207.

* DeGregori, Thomas R., 1989, "Out of Africa," *Priorities*, publication of American Council on Science and Health, Summer 1989.

* Goldstein, Robert and Betty Olson, "Applying Genetic Ecology to Environmental Management," *Journal of Environmental Science and Technology*, Vol. 22, No. 4, 1988, pp. 370–372.

(4) Whelan, Elizabeth, 1985, *Toxic Terror*, Jameson Books, Inc., 722 Columbus Street, Ottawa, IL 61350.

(5) Claus and Bolander, op. cit.

(6) Whelan, Elizabeth, 1985, *Toxic Terror*, footnote, p. 67, op. cit. In the footnote, Lamont Cole says, "To feed a starving child is to exacerbate the world population problem"; and Charles Wursta (chief scientist for the Environmental Defense Fund), says, referring to the banning of DDT, "this is as good a way to get rid of them as any." ("Them" refers to "all those little brown people in poor countries.")

(7) Whelan, Elizabeth, 1985, *Toxic Terror*, pp. 63–67 and pp. 73–85, op. cit.

* Isaac, Rael Jean and Erich Isaac, 1985, *The Coercive Utopians*, p. 70, Discipleship Books, Regnery Gateway, Inc., 1130 17th St., Washington, DC 20036.

* Efron, Edith, 1984, *The Apocalyptics*, Simon & Schuster, NY, pp. 31–33 and pp. 124–134.

(8) Edwards, J. Gordon, 1981, *Silent Spring—Broken Spring*, National Council for Environmental Balance, Louisville, KY 40207.

(9) Barrons, Keith C., 1981, *Are Pesticides Really Necessary?*, Regnery Gateway, Inc., 1130 17th St., Washington, DC 20036, p. 106ff.

* Whelan, *Toxic Terror*, op. cit.

(10) Whelan, *Toxic Terror*, op. cit., p. 85.

(11) Barrons, Keith C., 1988, *The Positive Side of Pesticides*, pp. 5–6, National Council for Environmental Balance, Louisville, KY 40207.

(12) Arnold, Ron, 1987, *Ecology Wars: Rethinking Environmentalism*, p. 12, Free Enterprise Press, 12500 NE 10th Place, Bellevue, WA 98005.

(13) Ames, Bruce N., 1985, in *Toxic Terror*, p. 128, op. cit.; also, "The State of Nature," *The Wall Street Journal*, 10 October 1989.

(14) Ames, Bruce N., 1989, "Pesticides, Risk, and Applesauce," *Science*, Vol. 244, pp. 755–757, 19 May 1989.

(15) Bradlee, Ben, 1989, reported by David Brooks in *The Wall Street Journal*, 5 October 1989, and, much earlier, by John J. McKetta of the National Council for Environmental Balance.

Chapter 7:   THE ALAR, ASBESTOS, PCB, AND DIOXIN SCARES

(1) Irvine, Reed, editor, 1989, *Confessions of a Radical Disinformer: The War on Alar*, Accuracy in Media, Inc., 1275 K Street NW, Suite 1150, Washington, DC 20005, XVIII, 20 October 1989.

(2) Melloan, George, 1989, *Food Scaremongers Are Beginning to Push Their Luck*; also, "The State of Nature," *The Wall Street Journal*, 10 October 1989.

(3) Knote, Charles, 1989, *The Amazing Truth About Pesticides' Safety*, Missouri Pest Control Association, Box 163, Cape Girardeau, MO 63701.

(4) Geranios, Nicholas K., 1989, "Alar-Troubled Growers May Give Away Apples," *Morning News Tribune*, Tacoma, Associated Press, 18 June 1989, and "Where Apples Redden, Never Pry", AP, Yakima, 24 October 1989.

* Koshland, Daniel E., 1989, "Scare of the Week," editorial in *Science*, Vol. 244, No. 4900, 7 April 1989.

* Hathaway, Jane, 1989, "Absolutely Anathema," *The Wall Street Journal*, 14 November 1989.

(5) Irvine, Reed, op. cit.

(6) Irvine, Reed, ibid.

(7) Ames, Bruce N., 1989, "Pesticides, Risk, and Applesauce," *Science*, Vol. 244, pp. 255–257, 19 May 1989.

* McGee, Harold, 1984, "The Nature of Plants" and "The Composition and Quality of Plants," in *On Food and Cooking*, Charles Scribner's Sons, NY, 1984; also, "The Story of Breakfast Cereals," p. 246ff, ibid.

(8) National Research Council, Board on Agriculture, *Alternative Agriculture*, National Academy Press, 1989.

* Barrons, Keith C., 1989, *Organic Farming: The Whole Story*, National Council for Environmental Balance, Louisville, KY 40207.

(9) Rousseau, Jean-Jacques, in *Emile*, 1762, quoted in McGee, op. cit, p. 525.

(10) McGee, op. cit., also p. 525.

(11) de Tocqueville, Alexis, 1830, quoted in *On Food and Cooking*, op. cit., p. 519.

(12) Franklin, Benjamin, 1691, quoted in *On Food and Cooking*, op. cit., p. 526.

(13) Japenza, Ann, 1989, *Livestock Liberation*, Harrowsmith, November/December 1989, pp. 34–43.

(14) Parfit, Michael, 1990, "Earth First!ers Wield a Mean Monkey Wrench," *Smithsonian*, Vol. 21, No. 1, April 1990, pp. 184–204.

(15) Brooks, David, 1990, "Saving the Earth From Its Friends: Environmentalists: High, Low, and Dangerous," *National Review*, Vol. XLII, No. 6, 1 April 1990, p. 28.

(16) *Ecodefense: A Field Guide to Monkeywrenching*, second edition, edited by Dave Foreman and Bill Haywood, Ned Ludd Books, Tucson, AZ, 1987.

(17) Mossman, B. T. et al, 1990, "Asbestos: Scientific Developments and Implications for Public Policy," *Science*, Vol. 247, pp. 294–301, 19 January 1990.

(18) Draft summary, *Estimates of the Fraction of Cancer Incidence in the U.S. Attributable to Occupational Factors*, NCI and National Institute of Environmental Health Sciences, 11 September 1978.

(19) Melloan, George, 1988, "A Company Held Captive by the Plaintiff Bar in Business World," *The Wall Street Journal*, 4 October 1988.

(20) Fumento, M., 1989, "The Asbestos Ripoff," *The American Spectator*, October 1989.

(21) Cairns, John, 1978, Conference on Cancer Prevention; Quantitative Aspects, sponsored by Director, NCI, 26 September 1978, Sheraton International Center, Reston, VA.

(22) Doll, Richard and Richard Peto, 1978, op. cit.

(23) Dunn, James R., 1985, *Asbestos: Let's Get the Facts Straight*, National Council on Environmental Balance, Louisville, KY 40207.

* Canadian Royal Commission on Asbestos, 1986, EPA hearings, Washington, DC, 15–17 October 1986.

* *New England Journal of Medicine*, 2 November 1989.

(24) Dunn, op. cit.

(25) Bennett, M. J., 1989, "Asbestos," in *Priorities*, American Council on Science and Health, NY 1989.

(26) "PCBs: Mad Dog of the Environment?," Chapter 5, *Toxic Terror*, Whelan, op. cit.

* Napier, Kristine, 1988, "The Mythical Monsters," American Council on Science and Health, *News and Views*, March/April 1988, pp. 3–4.

* *PCBs: Is the Cure Worth the Cost?*, American Council on Science and Health booklet, 1987.

* Beckmann, Petr, 1985–86, "EPA Bans PCB; Causes Transformer Fires," *Access to Energy*, March 1984 and Vol. 16, No. 4, December 1988.

(27) "The Yusho Disease Episode," Whelan, op. cit., p. 142.

(28) Douglas, John, "Genetic Ecology in Action," *EPRI Journal*, September 1988, pp. 15–21.

(29) "Deadly Dioxin," ibid, Chapter 8.

* Reggani, G., 1981, *TCDD, Formation, Occurrence, Toxicology, Regulatory Toxicology, and Pharmacology*, 1:212, 1981.

(30) Letts, Roger W. M., 1986, *Dioxin in the Environment: Its Effect on Human Health*, report by American Council on Science and Health.

(31) Havender, W. R., 1981, "Science vs. Politics in Regulatory Washington," *The American Spectator*, June 1981.

Chapter 8:   RADIATION AROUND US

(1) Cobb, Charles E., Jr., 1989, "Living With Radiation," *National Geographic*, April 1989, pp. 403–437.

* Eisenbud, Merrill, 1987, *Environmental Radioactivity From Natural Industrial and Military Sources*, Academic Press, 1250 Sixth Avenue, San Diego, CA 97101.

* Wagner, Henry N., Jr., and Linda E. Ketchum, *Living With Radiation—The Risk, The Promise*, Johns Hopkins University Press, 701 West 40th Street, Baltimore, MD 21211.

* Moghissi, A. Alan, editor, 1978, *Radioactivity in Consumer Products*, USNRC, NUREG/CP-0003.

* Cohen, Bernard L., 1981, "How Dangerous Is Radiation?," *AECL Ascent*, Vol. 2, No. 4, 1981, pp. 8–12.

* Cohen, Bernard L., 1982, "The Genetic Effects of Natural Radiation," *AECL Ascent*, Vol. 3, No. 3, 1982, pp. 8–13.

(2) Beckmann, Petr, 1986, "Iodine 131 and Chernobyl," *The American Spectator*, July 1986.

(3) Marshall, Walter (Lord Marshall of Goring), 1986, "Nuclear Power: Energy of Today and Tomorrow," ENC International Conference, 2 June 1986.

(4) Young, Alvin L. and George P. Dix, 1988, "The Federal Approach to Radiation Issues," *Environmental Science and Technology*, Vol. 22, No. 7, pp. 733–739.

* Grant, R. W., 1988, "Radiation Exposure by Source," in *Trashing Nuclear Power*, p. 33ff, Quandary House, Box 773, Manhattan Beach, CA 90266.

(5) Luckey, T. D., 1980, *Hormesis and Ionizing Radiation*, p. 16, CRC Press, Inc., 2000 NW 24th Street, Boca Raton, FL 33431.

* Eisenbud, Merrill, 1987, op. cit., p. 160.

* Lapp, Ralph E., 1979, *The Radiation Controversy*, Reddy Communications, Inc., 537 Steamboat Road, Greenwich, CT 06830.

* Cohen, Bernard L., 1983, *Before It's Too Late*, see especially Chapter 2, "How Dangerous Is Radiation?," Plenum Press, New York and London.

* Beckmann, Petr, 1990, "Death From Outer Space," *Access to Energy*, Vol. 17, No. 8, 1990.

(6) Cohen, Bernard L., *Before It's Too Late*, 1983, op. cit.

* Luckey, T. D., 1980, op. cit.

(7) Beckmann, Petr, 1982, *Access to Energy*, Vol. 9, No. 5, Box 2298, Boulder, CO 80306.

(8) Eisenbud, Merrill, 1987, op. cit.

* Beckmann, Petr, 1985, *The Health Hazards of NOT Going Nuclear*, Golem Press, Box 1342, Boulder, CO 80306.

* Cohen, Bernard L., 1988, *Health Effects of Low Level Radiation*, report from American Council on Science and Health, 47 Maple Street, Summit, NJ 07901.

(9) Eisenbud, Merrill, 1987, op. cit.

(10) Ibid.

(11) Cohen, Bernard L., 1983, op. cit.

(12) Pirchman, A, 1932, "Working Miners and Lung Cancer at Joachinosthal," *American Journal of Cancer*, 1932.

(13) Ray, D. L., 1986, "Who Is Radon and Why Are His Daughters So Bad?," *World Media Report*, Winter 1986.

* Thomas, Ron, 1989, "Radon's Troublesome Daughters Stir Up Controversy," *AECL Ascent*, Vol. 8, No. 2, summer 1989.

188   NOTES

* Brookes, Warren T., 1989, "Radon Terrorism Unleashed by EPA," *The Washington Times*, 29 June 1989.

* Brookes, Warren T., 1990, "Radon: Anatomy of Risk-Hype," *The Detroit News*, 5 March 1990.

(14) Nero, A. V. et al, 1986, "Distribution of Radon 222: Concentrations in U.S. Homes," *Science*, 21 November 1986, pp. 992–997.

* Nero, A. V., 1988, "Controlling Indoor Pollution," *Scientific American*, May 1988.

* Lapp, R. E., 1989, *Radon Health Effects?*, radon panel, Health Physics Society meeting, Albuquerque, NM, 29 June 1989.

(15) Jenkins, Judge Bruce S., 1984, *Radiation Exposures in Utah From Bomb Tests*, 1951–62, decision in Federal Court.

(16) Brundage, J. F. et al, 1988, "Building-Associated Risk of Febrile Acute Respiratory Illness in Army Trainees," *Journal of the American Medical Association*, 8 April 1988, pp. 2108–2112.

* Marcus, Amy Dockser, 1989, "In Some Workplaces, Ill Winds Blow," *The Wall Street Journal*, 9 October 1989.

* Lawrence, Henry J., 1989, "Is Your Office Out to Kill You?," *Seattle Post-Intelligencer*, 14 August 1989.

* Holzman, David, 1989, "Elusive Culprits in Workplace Ills," *Insight*, 26 June 1989.

(17) Efron, Edith, 1984, *The Apocalyptics*, Chapter 12, "The Case of the Missing Thresholds," p. 344, Simon & Schuster, Inc., Rockefeller Center, 1230 Avenue of the Americas, NY 10020.

* Luckey, T. D., 1980, *Radiation Hormesis*, op. cit.

(18) Ibid.

* Sagan, Leonard A., 1987, "What Is Hormesis and Why Haven't We Heard About It Before?," *Health Physics*, guest editorial, Vol. 52, No. 5, pp. 521–525, May 1987.

* Cohen, Bernard L., 1987, "Tests of the Linear No Threshold Dose Response Relationship for High LET Radiation," *Health Physics*, Vol. 52, No. 5, pp. 629–636, May 1989.

* Fremlin, J., 1989, "Radiation Hormesis," *Atom*, London, April 1989.

* Luckey, T. D., 1988, "Hormesis and Nurture With Ionizing Radiation," in *Global 2000 Revisited*, Hugh Ellsaesser, editor, Paragon House publication, 1988.

(19) Letter from Marshall Brucer to *Time* magazine, quoted in *Access to Energy*, Vol. 16, No. 7, March 1989.

(20) Luckey, T. D., 1988, op. cit.

(21) Fleck, C. M., H. Oberhummer and W. Hofmann, 1987, *Inference of Chemically and Radiologically Induced Cancer at Environmental Doses*, Fourth International Symposium on the Natural Radiation Environment, Lisbon, Portugal, 7–11 December 1987.

(22) Cohen, Bernard L., 1989, "Lung Cancer and Radon: Hormesis at Low Levels of Exposure in American Homes," *Access to Energy*, Vol. 16, No. 9, 1989.

* Cohen, Bernard L., 1989, "Expected Indoor Radon-222 Levels in Counties With Very High and Very Low Lung Cancer Rates," *Health Physics*, Vol. 57, No. 6, December 1989, pp. 897–906.

Chapter 9: NUCLEAR MEDICINE

(1) Blahd, William H., 1971, *Nuclear Medicine*, second edition, McGraw Hill Book Co., New York, 820 pages.

* Wagner, Henry N., Jr., editor, *Principles of Nuclear Medicine*, W. B. Saunders Co., Philadelphia, 858 pages.

* *Highly recommended:* For a comprehensive, nontechnical discussion, see "Medicine's New Vision," by Howard Sochurek, 1987, *National Geographic*, January 1987, pp. 2–40.

(2) Harby, Karla, 1988, *Newsline: Journal of Nuclear Medicine*, Vol. 29, No. 3, March 1988, pp. 283–86.

(3) Smith, Steven R., 1982, "The View Inside: Medical Diagnosis Through Nuclear Medicine," *AECL Ascent*, Vol. 3, No. 2, 1982, pp. 2–9.

* Holzman, David, 1989, "Seeing Is Healing: Imaging Unveils Medical Mysteries," *Insight*, 16 October 1989, pp. 8–16.

* Evans, David, 1985, "Radioisotopes: AECL's Bread and Butter Business," *AECL Ascent*, winter 1984–85.

(4) "Keeping Cancer at Bay," Life Sciences section, *AECL Ascent*, Winter 1982–83, pp. 24–27.

(5) Brugger, R. M., 1987, *Highlights of MURR Accomplishments and University of Missouri Research Reactor*, annual report, July 1988–July 1989.

* Kowalsky, R. J. and J. R. Perry, 1987, *Radiopharmaceuticals in Nuclear Medicine Practice*, Appleton Lange, Norwalk, CT.

(6) Young, Alvin L. and George P. Dix, 1988, "The Federal Approach to Radiation Issues," *Environmental Science and Technology*, Vol. 22, No. 7, 1988, pp. 733–739.

* Battelle Memorial Institute, Pacific Northwest Laboratory, 1989, *Projection of Needs for Gamma Radiation Sources and Other Radioisotopes* *and Assessment of Alternative for Providing Radiation Sources*, PNL-6250, June 1989.

* Masefield, John, 1983, "Isomedix, Inc.: Penetrating Sterilization Markets With Gamma Rays," *AECL Ascent*, Summer 1983, pp. 27–29.

(7) Ibid, p. 27.

(8) Friedman, Stanton, 1985, "Pie in the Sky," *AECL Ascent*, Winter 1984–85, pp. 19–20.

(9) Special Report: Cover Story, 1985, "A New Era in Food Preservation Is Coming," *AECL Ascent*, Vol. 6, No. 1, pp. 5–16, 1985.

* Bee, Jim, editor, 1987, "Complex Issues: Food Irradiation," *AECL Ascent*, Vol. 7, No. 1, p. 3, 1987.

(10) Welt, Martin A., 1988, "Food Irradiation, a Weapon in the Arsenal Against Hunger," Executive Intelligence Review, *Science and Technology*, 7 October 1988.

(11) Wedekind, Lothar, 1986, "Can Food Irradiation Boost Nutrition in China?," *AECL Ascent*, Vol. 6, No. 3, pp. 21–23.

* Schwiegert, Bernard S. et al, 1988, third edition, *Irradiated Food*, report by American Council on Science and Health, pp. 1–35, 1995 Broadway, 18th floor, New York 10023.

* Truswell, A. Stewart, 1987, "Food Irradiation," *British Medical Journal*, Vol. 294, No. 6585, pp. 1437–8.

(12) Plutonium in RTGs, "Power for Satellites," *Access to Energy*, Vol. 17, No. 2, October 1989.

* DOE, SP–100 GES Program Office, Washington, DC 20545, *Space Reactor Safety*, Report DEP/NE052 (GTN), 1989.

* Truscello, V. C. and H. S. Davis, 1984, "Nuclear Electric Power in Space," *IEEE Spectrum*, December 1984.

(13) Jensen, George A. et al, 1987, "Radioluminescent Lights Score High in VFR Night Air Taxi Tests," *Northern Engineer*, Vol. 19, No. 1, Spring 1987.

(14) U.S. Department of Energy report: *Radioisotopes: Today's Applications*, 1988, DOE/NE 0089 ENERGY, PO Box 62, Oak Ridge, TN 37830.

* Friedman, Stanton, 1984, "What Does Nuclear Technology Have to Do With Pool Cues, Cow Fat, and Art Fakes?," Part 1, *AECL Ascent*, Spring 1984, pp. 14–18; Part 2, *AECL Ascent*, Summer 1984, pp. 15–17.

Chapter 10:   POWER FROM THE ATOM, THE SUN, AND THE WIND

(1) DuPont, Robert L., 1980, *Nuclear Phobia—Phobic Thinking About Nuclear Power*, Media Institute, 1627 K Street NW, Suite 201, Washington, DC 20006, 1980, 29 pages.

(2) Beckmann, Petr, 1979, *The Health Hazards of NOT Going Nuclear*, Golem Press, Box 1342, Boulder, CO 80306.

* Cohen, Bernard L., 1983, *Before It's Too Late: A Scientist's Case FOR Nuclear Power*, Plenum Publishing, 233 Spring Street, New York 10013.

* Grant, R. W., 1988, *Trashing Nuclear Power*, Quandary House, Box 773, Manhattan Beach, CA 90266.

* Jeffs, Eric, 1981, "Nuclear Power: A Route Out of World Crisis," *AECL Ascent*, Vol. 2, No. 3, 1981, pp. 10–13.

* McCracken, Samuel, 1982, *The War Against the Atom*, Basic Books, Inc., New York.

(3) Reports from U.S. Council on Energy Awareness, PO Box 66103, Dept. P.C. 14, Washington, DC 20035.

(4) Bee, Jim, 1988, editorial, "The Battle for Public Acceptance," *AECL Ascent*, Vol. 7, No. 3, p. 3.

* "International Atomic Energy Agency Reports: Nuclear Share of World Electricity Production Rises," 1988, in *AECL Ascent*, Vol. 7, No. 3, p. 30.

* Cohen, Karl, 1984, "Nuclear Power," Chapter 14, in *The Resourceful Earth*, editors Julian L. Simon and Herman Kahn, Basil Blackwell, Inc., 432 Park Avenue South, Suite 1505, New York 10016.

* IAEA, *Newsbriefs*, 1989, "Nuclear Share of Electricity Rises in 1988," Vol. 4, No. 4 (35), May 1989.

(5) Wargo, J. R., 1988, "Here They Come Again: A Wretched Win-Loss Record Fails to Daunt the Opposition," *Nuclear Industry*, March/April 1988, pp. 62–66.

* *The Comparative Risks of Different Methods of Generating Electricity*, policy statement of American Nuclear Society, ANS Document PPS-3, October 1979.

* *Energy and the Environment*, 1989, general position paper of American Society of Mechanical Engineers, July 1989.

(6) Cohen, Bernard L., 1990, *The Nuclear Energy Option: The Alternative for the 1990s*, in press, Plenum Publishing, 233 Spring Street, New York 10013.

(7) McGaw, Jim, 1989, "Energy and the Environment: A Precarious Balance; What Are the Alternatives?," *AECL Ascent*, Vol. 8, No. 1, Spring 1989, p. 27.

* Burge, Raymond, 1988, "Tracking Alternative Energy Sources," *AECL Ascent*, Vol. 7, No. 3, 1988.

* Beckmann, Petr, 1979, *Why "Soft" Technologies Will Not Be America's Energy Salvation*, Golem Press, Box 1342, Boulder, CO 80306.

* Beckmann, Petr, 1984, "Solar Energy and Other 'Alternative' Energy Sources," in *The Resourceful Earth*, Chapter 15A & B, pp. 415–438, Basil Blackwell, Inc., 432 Park Avenue South, Suite 1505, New York 10016.

* Cohen, Bernard L., 1983, "The Solar Dream," Chapter 9, p. 241, in *Before It's Too Late*, Plenum Publishing, 233 Spring Street, New York 10013.

(8) Moore, Taylor, 1989, "Thin Films: Expanding the Solar Marketplace," *EPRI Journal*, March 1989, pp. 4–15.

* Beckmann, Petr, 1980, "Solar Electricity and Economics," *Access to Energy*, Vol. 7, No. 7, March 1980.

* Grant, R. W., 1988, "The Solar Alternative?," in *Trashing Nuclear Power*, p. 88, Quandary House, Box 773, Manhattan Beach, CA 90266.

* Inhaber, Herbert, 1979, "Risk With Energy From Conventional and Non-Conventional Sources," *Science*, Vol. 203, 23 February 1979, pp. 718–723.

* "Medical Perspective on Nuclear Power," 1989, Council Report, *Journal of the American Medical Association*, Vol. 262, No. 19, 17 November 1989, pp. 2724–29.

(9) Grant, op. cit., p. 91.

* Beckmann, Petr, 1982, "Solar Electricity: SOLAR ONE," *Access to Energy*, Vol. 9, No. 10, June 1982.

(10) "Fire in Southern California Edison's SOLAR ONE," *Access to Energy*, Vol. 17, No. 7, March 1990.

(11) Grant, R. W., op. cit., p. 90.

(12) Beckmann, Petr, 1979, *Why "Soft" Technologies Will Not Be America's Energy Salvation*, op. cit., p. 2.

(13) Cohen, Bernard L., 1983, "The Solar Dream," Chapter 9, in *Before It's Too Late*, op. cit.

(14) Inhaber, Herbert, 1983, *Energy Risk Assessment*, Gordon & Breach, 1 Park Avenue, New York 10016.

* "Building Material Production," in *The War Against the Atom*, Basic Books, Inc., Chapter 4, p. 86.

(15) MacIntyre, Linden, 1981, "Wind Power, Applications in the Gulf of St. Lawrence," *AECL Ascent*, Vol. 3, No. 1, 1981, pp. 8–13.

* Schaefer, John, 1989, "Wind Systems," *EPRI Journal*, July/August 1989, pp. 49–51.

(16) Reported in *Access to Energy*, Vol. 11, No. 2, October 1983.

(17) *Access to Energy*, Vol. 10, No. 12, August 1983.

(18) *Access to Energy*, Vol. 3, No. 10, October, 1976.

(19) *Access to Energy*, Vol. 7, No. 7, March 1980.

(20) Ackerman, Bruce A. and W. T. Hassler, 1981, *Clean Coal, Dirty Air*, Yale University Press, 92-A Yale Station, New Haven, CT 06520.

* Beckmann, Petr, 1979, *The Non-Problem of Nuclear Wastes*, Golem Press, Box 1342, Boulder, CO 80306.

* Wilson, R., S. D. Colome, J. D. Spengler, and D. G. Wilson, 1980, *Health Effects of Fossil Fuel Burning*, Ballinger Publishing, Cambridge, MA.

* Cohen, Bernard L., 1990, "Hazards of High Level Radioactive Waste—the Great Myth," Chapter 11, in *The Nuclear Option: The Alternative for the 1990s*, in press, Plenum Publishing, New York.

(21) Vecsey, G. and Doroszlai, P. G. K., 1987, *A Simple New Heating Reactor of High Inherent Safety*, typewritten report presented at joint meeting of American Nuclear Society and Swiss Section of Nuclear Society, Public Forum, Nuclear Energy Today and Tomorrow, Zurich, Switzerland, August 1987.

(22) Duffy, John Q., 1981, "Slowpoke: The Little Reactor That Can," *AECL Ascent*, Vol. 3, No. 1, 1983, pp. 22–26.

* Kay, R. E. and J. W. Hilborn, "Slowpoke: A Demonstration of Simplified Reactor Control and Unattended Operation," *ANS Transactions*, Vol. 17, 1973, p. 453 and pp. 481–482.

* Lotz, Jim, 1987, "Dalhousie's Little Reactor," *AECL Ascent*, Vol. 7, No. 2, p. 10.

* "Nuclear District Heating," in *Secure Booklet* by ASEA-ATOM, Box 53, S-721, Vasteras, Sweden.

* Golay, Michael W. and Neil E. Todreas, 1990, "Advanced Light Water Reactors," *Scientific American*, Vol. 262, No. 4, April 1990, pp. 82–89.

* Fisher, Arthur, 1990, "Next Generation Nuclear Reactors: Dare We Build Them?," *Popular Science*, April 1990, pp. 68–77.

(23) Warren, Anita, 1989, "That Powerless Feeling," *Nuclear Industry*, first quarter 1989, pp. 10–17.

* Ray, Dixy Lee, 1988, "Why Doesn't the Public See It the Way We Do?," proceedings of International Conference on Enhanced Safety of Nuclear Reactors, School of Engineering and Applied Science, George Washington University, August 1988.

* Cherner, Sara, 1988, "Yeoman Service: They Say Good News Is Not News; That's Why You Don't Hear Much About Nuclear Plants That Perform Well," *Nuclear Industry*, July/August, 1988, pp. 34–40.

(24) Myers, Richard, editor, "Quick Fix for the 1990s," *Nuclear Industry*, third quarter, 1989, pp. 5–7.

(25) Cohen, Bernard L., 1983, "Costs of Nuclear Power," Chapter 8, in *Before It's Too Late*, op. cit, p. 217ff.

    * Warren, Anita, 1989, "Nuclear Glasnost: For the First Time There's a Safety Net Under the World's Nuclear Power Plants," *Nuclear Industry*, second quarter 1989, p. 3.

(26) Executive Summary, proceedings of the International Conference on Enhanced Safety of Nuclear Reactors, 1988, George Washington University, op. cit., see also individual papers.

(27) Cohen, Bernard L., 1990, "Spending Money to Reduce Risks," in *The Nuclear Energy Option*, op. cit., in press.

(28) Bisconti, Ann S. and Robert Livingston, 1989, "Simple Designs, Simple Words," *Nuclear Industry*, third quarter 1989, pp. 10–13.

    * Livingston, Robert, 1988, "The Next Generation," *Nuclear Industry*, July/August 1988, pp. 18–33.

(29) Catron, Jack, 1989, "New Interest in Passive Reactor Designs," *EPRI Journal*, April/May 1989, pp. 5–13.

    * Ryan, Margaret L. et al, *Outlook on Advanced Reactors*, special report to readers of *Nucleonics Week*, 30 March 1989.

    * Devine, Jack, 1988, "Advanced Light Water Reactors," proceedings of the International Conference on Advanced Safety of Nuclear Reactors, op. cit., p. 77.

(30) Hannerz, Kare, 1988, *Pius Reactor*, in proceedings on Enhanced Safety of Nuclear Reactors, School of Engineering and Applied Science, Institute for Technology and Strategic Research, George Washington University, Washington, DC, ITSR Report, No. 008.

(31) Blue, Linden S., 1988, *Modular HTGR*, ibid, p. 94.

(32) Till, Charles S., 1988, *Integral Fast Reactor*, ibid, p. 94.

(33) Revesz, Zsolt, 1988, *Geyser Reactor*, ibid, p. 125.

(34) Kirchner, Walter L., 1988, *Compact Nuclear Power Source*, Los Alamos National Laboratory, 8 January 1988, pp. 1–39.

Chapter 11: NUCLEAR WASTE

(1) By far the best, most up to date, complete, and accurate discussion of nuclear waste in all its ramifications will be found in Chapters 11 and 12 of Bernard L. Cohen's new book (1990), *The Nuclear Option: The Alternative for the 1990s*, Plenum Publishing, 233 Spring Street, New York 10013.

(2) "Waste Management Update," 1988, special section in *Nuclear News*, ANS publication, Vol. 31, No. 3, March 1988, pp. 42–85.

(3) Lilienthal, David E., 1964, *The Journals of David E. Lilienthal*, Vol. II, *The Atomic Energy Years, 1945–50*, Harper & Row, New York.

(4) Ray, Dixy Lee and Anibal L. Taboas, 1983, *Waste Management: The Missing Link*, DOE Defense Waste and Byproducts Management Conference, Washington, DC.

* Hewlett, R. G. and F. Duncan, 1969, *The Atomic Shield, 1947–52*, Vol. II of the history of the U.S. Atomic Energy Commission, Penn State University Press.

(5) Beckmann, Petr, 1979, *The Non-Problem of Nuclear Wastes*, Golem Press, Box 1342, Boulder, CO 80306.

(6) Wagner, Henry N. and Linda E. Ketchum, 1989, "Nuclear Waste Disposal: Not in My Backyard," see especially p. 129 in *Living With Radiation: The Risk, the Promise*, Johns Hopkins University Press, Baltimore.

(7) Marshall, Walter, Lord Goring, 1988, in *Access to Energy*, Vol. 16, No. 1, 1988.

(8) Horwitz, E. Philip, 1986, "New Radioactive Waste Treatment Could Save Taxpayers Billions," Logos, Argonne National Laboratory, *Progress Through Science*, Vol. 4, No. 3, Autumn 1986, pp. 6–9.

(9) Doncals, R. A., J. E. Schmidt, and R. W. Rathbun, with E. Rodwell, 1988, *Transmutation of Nuclear Waste*, Westinghouse Electric Corporation and EPRI Journal, typewritten manuscript only.

* Beckmann, Petr, 1988, in *Access to Energy*.

(10) Burge, Ray, 1989, "The Environmental Case for Nuclear Power," *AECL Ascent*, Vol. 8, No. 1, Spring 1989, p. 14.

(11) Ray, Dixy Lee, 1986, "Nuclear Waste: What Good Is It?," paper presented at Nuclear Waste Symposium, published in *Tennessee Law Review*, Vol. 53, No. 3, Spring 1986.

* Ray, Dixy Lee, 1988, "Waste Not," *Nuclear and Chemical Waste Management*, Vol. 8, pp. 91–95, 1988.

(12) Cohen, Bernard L., 1984, "The Hazards of Nuclear Power: High Level Waste," in *The Resourceful Earth*, op. cit., p. 555.

* Gertz, Carl P., 1989, "Yucca Mountain, Nevada: Is It a Safe Place for Isolation of High Level Radioactive Waste?," *Journal of the Institute of Nuclear Materials Management*, Vol. XVII, No. 3, April 1989.

(13) Ostenberg, Charles L., 1986, "Basic Factors Affecting the Land; Fresh Water vs. the Sea Option for Waste Disposal," in *The Role of the Oceans as a Waste Disposal Option*, G. Kullenberg, editor, D. Reidel Publishing, 1986, pp. 39–53.

* Ostenberg, Charles L., 1986, "Old Submarines and Ocean Dumping Policy," *Marine Policy Reports*, University of Delaware, College of Marine Sciences, Vol. 8, No. 5, March 1986.

* Ostenberg, Charles L., 1985, "Waste Disposal: Where Should It Be? Land or Sea?," Communications, *The Siren*, No. 28, May 1985.

(14) Report on Sub-Sea Bed Disposal of Radioactive Wastes, Sandia National Laboratory, 1981.

* Miles, Edward L., Kai N. Lee, and Elaine M. Carlin, 1985, *Nuclear Waste Disposal Under the Sea Bed: Assessing the Policy Issues*, Institute of International Studies, University of California at Berkeley, No. 22, 1985.

(15) Ray, Roger et al, 1987, *The Natural History of Eniwetok Atoll*, Vol. 1, *The Ecosystem, Environments, Biotas, and Processes*, DOE/EV/00703-TI, Vol. 1 (DE87006110).

Chapter 12: ENVIRONMENTALISM AND THE FUTURE

(1) Ray, Dixy Lee, 1989, "The Greenhouse Blues; Keeping Cool About Global Warming," *Policy Review*, Summer 1989, pp. 70–72.

* Ray, Dixy Lee, 1990, "Global Warming: What's Known and What Is Not Known," *The Washington Times*, 22 April 1990.

(2) Tucker, William, 1982, *Progress and Privilege: America in the Age of Environmentalism*, Anchor Press, Doubleday, Garden City, NY.

(3) Arnold, Ron, 1987, *Ecology Wars: Environmentalism As If People Mattered*, Free Enterprise Press, Bellevue, WA, 1987.

* Arnold, Ron, 1982, *At the Eye of the Storm: James Watt and the Environmentalists*, Regnery Gateway, 1130 17th St., Washington, DC 20036.

(4) Simon, Julian L. and Herman Kahn, 1984, introduction to *The Resourceful Earth: A Response to Global 2000*, Basil Blackwell, 432 Park Avenue, Suite 1505, New York 10016.

(5) Brand, Stewart, *Whole Earth Catalogue*.

(6) Foreman, Dave, 1987, *Ecodefense: A Field Guide to Monkeywrenching*, Ned Ludd Books, PO Box 5871, Tucson, AZ 85703.

(7) *Ecotage*, 1987, see *Ecodefense*, second edition, ibid.

(8) Watson, Paul (founder of Greenpeace), 1982, in *Access to Energy*, Vol. 10, No. 4, December 1982.

(9) Lovejoy, Thomas, 1989, quoted by David Brooks in *The Wall Street Journal* article, "Journalists and Others for Saving the Planet."

(10) Schell, Jonathan, 1987, "Our Fragile Earth," *Discover*, October 1987, p. 47.

(11) Benedick, Richard, 1989, "Who Needs Evidence?," in a Special

Report: "The Greenhouse Effect Is a Fraud," by Rogelio A. Maduro, *21st Century*, March/April 1989, pp. 14–15 and p. 25.

(12) Schneider, Stephen, quoted in "Our Fragile Earth," op. cit.

(13) GAP in Isaac, Jean Rael, 1985, "Games Anti-Nukes Play: The Government Accountability Project's Assault on Nuclear Energy, *The American Spectator*, Vol. 18, No. 11, November 1985, p. 10ff.

(14) Caldicott, Helen, 1985, in *Toxic Terror*, by Elizabeth Whelan, Jameson Books, Ottawa, IL, pp. 53–54.

* Caldicott, Helen, 1982, in *Doctors Against Health*, by Petr Beckmann, Golem Press, Box 1342, Boulder, CO 80306.

* Ehrlich, Paul, Anne H. Ehrlich, and John P. Holdren, 1977, *Ecoscience: Population, Resources, Environment*, Freeman, San Francisco.

(15) Ehrlich, Paul, 1989, quoted in article by David Brooks, "Journalists and Others for Saving the Planet," *The Wall Street Journal*, op. cit; also in *The Apocalyptics*, by Edith Efron, 1984, pp. 33–35.

(16) Boulding, Kenneth, 1982, in *Progress and Privilege*, by William Tucker, pp. 105–6.

(17) Earth First! Newsletter, referenced in *Access to Energy*, Vol. 17, No. 4, December 1989.

(18) Brower, David, in *The Coercive Utopians*, by Rael Jean Isaac and Erich Isaac, 1985, Regnery Gateway, Inc., 1130 17th St., Washington, DC 20036.

(19) Prince Philip, 1989, in Rep. Claudine Schneider's "The Greenhouse Effect Hoax: Legislation in Washington," Special Report, *Executive Intelligence Review*, PO Box 17390, Washington, DC 10041–0390, p. 28–29 and p. 127.

(20) *The Economist*, London, editorial, 28 December 1988, subtitled "Dinosaurs and Destiny."

(21) Amery, Carl, quoted in *Mensch & Energie*, April 1983.

(22) Gore, Senator Albert, 1989, calls for "International Year of Greenhouse Effect," in *Special Report*, op. cit., p. 14, pp. 69–74, pp. 96–103, and pp. 113–116.

(23) Zaragoza, Federico Mayor, director general, UNESCO, in *Science and Technology*, E/R, April 1989, p. 26.

(24) Schneider, Claudine, 1989, op. cit, p. 15, pp. 69–74, and pp. 104–113.

(25) Leahy, Pat, and Jim Jeffords, senators from Vermont, ibid, p. 70.

(26) Suggested by comments in Florman, Samuel C., 1976, *The Existential Pleasures of Engineering*, St. Martin's Press, 175 Fifth Avenue, New York 10010, p. 145.

For additional reading:

* Mandel, Susan, 1990, "Funding the Usual Suspects," *National Review*, 19 March 1990, p. 26.

* Horowitz, David, 1990, "Making the Green One Red," *National Review*, 19 March 1990, pp. 39–40.

INDEX

199

California, 59, 131–32
Canada, 25, 56, 62–63, 66–67, 124, 134, 141
cancer, 6, 18, 47, 76; asbestos, 83, 85; dioxin, 89; PCB, 86, 88; and nuclear medicine, 115–16; radiation, 98–99, 102–03, 106, 111–12
Cape Matatula, 54
Carbon-14, 40–41, 97, 146
carbon dating, 40
carbon dioxide, 5–7, 32, 34–37, 41–43, 52–53, 67, 124–25, 133, 161
carbon disulfide, 58
carbon monoxide, 37
carbon sulfide, 58
carbonic acid, 52
carcinogens, 5–6, 73, 77, 83, 89, 124
Carson, Rachel, 70
Carter, President Jimmy, 151–52
Castro, Fidel, 167
catalytic converter, 61
cement industry, 56
Central America, 58
Central Electricity Generating Board, 96, 147
cesium (Cesium-137), 120, 150, 155
charcoal, 20, 26, 128
Chernobyl, 96, 125
Chicago Tribune, The, 90
China, 55, 119
chlorine, 46
chloroflourocarbon (CFC), 45–47, 167
chromium, 76, 130
Churchill, Winston, 143
Clean Air Act of 1970, 58, 65–66
climate, 39–40, 42, 53, 61
CMPO, 149
coal, xvi, 15, 20, 42, 55–56, 61, 65–67, 125, 128–30, 133–35, 147
Cobalt-60, 115, 117
Coghill and Likens report, 53
Cohen, Dr. Bernard L., 112
Colorado Public Service, 138
Columbia River, 155
Commoner, Barry, 12
Communicable Disease Center of the U.S. Health Service, 69
Compact Nuclear Power Source (CNPS), 140
concrete, 130

Congress, 65–66, 136, 155, 169–70
Congressional Joint Committee on Atomic Energy, 144
Conservation Foundation, 167
copper, 130
"Critical Mass" conference, 123
Cuba, 167
Cuyahoga River, 164
Czechoslovakia, 102, 124

D

Davis, Jackson, 154
DDT, 68–74
deforestation, 35–36
Department of Defense, 136
Department of Energy, 145, 155
Department of Health, Education and Welfare (HEW), 83–84
Department of State, 167
diesel power, 25
dioxin, 3–4, 74, 88–91
DNA, 76
Doll, Richard, 84
Draft Summary of 1978, 84

E

Earth First!, 81–82, 163, 166, 168
East Germany, 125
Ecotage, 166
Eddy, Dr. John, 40–41
Edison Electric Institute, 27
Edison, Thomas, 20
Ehrlich, Paul, 12, 72, 168
Eisenhower, Dwight D., 113
El Chicon, 37–38
El Nino, 35
electricity, 20–21, 23, 25–27; cost of, 88; production of, 42, 61, 109, 123–25, 128–32; nuclear generated, 136–41, 143–44, 151–52
Emergency Core Cooling System (ECCS), 126
encephalitis, 70
energy, 12–13, 25
England, 50, 64, 66, 96, 100, 111
Environmental Defense Fund, 71, 73
Environmental Protection Agency (EPA), xv, 3–6, 162; acid rain, 49, 64; Alar,